The Church Growth Handbook

Includes Complete Ministry Audit

William M. Easum

ABINGDON PRESS / NASHVILLE

CHURCH GROWTH HANDBOOK

Copyright © 1990 by Abingdon Press

This book is printed on acid-free paper.

COVER DESIGN BY
JOHN R. ROBINSON

Library of Congress Cataloging-in-Publication Data

EASUM, WILLIAM M., 1939–
  The church growth handbook / William M. Easum.
    p.   cm.

  ISBN 0-687-08161-0 (alk. paper)

  1. Church growth—Handbooks, manuals, etc. I. Title.
  BV652.25.E37   1990   89-38790
  254'.5—dc20   CIP

Scripture quotations are from the Revised Standard Version of the Bible,
copyright 1946, 1952, 1971 by the Division of Christian Education of the
National Council of Churches of Christ in the USA. Used by permission.

See Acknowledgments for credit to *The United Methodist Reporter* of Dallas,
Texas.

MANUFACTURED IN THE UNITED STATES OF AMERICA

FOREWORD

Get ready for an adventure! Bill Easum has written one of the most practical and helpful books on holistic church growth to be published in recent years. The author's insights come from years of experience as pastor of a dynamic, growing congregation, and he has shared those insights in seminars attended by hundreds of pastors and lay people from major denominations. The *Church Growth Handbook* allows the reader to join those seminars and receive insights and observations that will make a difference in any local church.

Few pastors are able to conceptualize and communicate growth principles as clearly as Bill Easum does. I found myself taking notes, underlining sentences, and turning pages with growing interest.

An occasional reader might say, "Well, this could happen in Texas or in the Bible Belt, but my situation is different." I was amazed to discover that the same basic priorities and approaches to ministry and mission that helped Colonial Hills Church grow in San Antonio helped Central Church maintain vital growth and ministry in Richland, Washington.

I would encourage every pastor and lay person interested in Growth Plus to read Easum's book. You may not agree with everything he says, but you will be challenged, confronted, disturbed, and inspired. And you will see new possibilities for effective growth in your church.

Joe Harding

Section on Evangelism
General Board of Discipleship
The United Methodist Church

Used properly, this handbook will help congregations do two things: first, accurately identify their strengths and weaknesses; second, develop strategies to overcome their weaknesses and further develop their strengths.

Chapters 1 through 6 present background material for the Ministry Audit in chapter 7. The Ministry Audit is designed to be used only after a thorough reading of those chapters, which will guide the leaders of your church in gathering the information asked for in the Ministry Audit.

Before reaching conclusions on each of the growth principles, church leaders may find it helpful to reread each section. The effectiveness of the Ministry Audit will depend on how closely your conclusions follow the recommendations of this handbook.

Church leaders are always encouraged to secure the services of a competent consultant, especially when attempting to steer a congregation in new directions. Many consulting organizations are now available to help your church. The author of this handbook is also available if you write to him directly at 5247 Vance Jackson, San Antonio, Texas 78230.

CONTENTS

ACKNOWLEDGMENTS

This book is the result of a labor of love between a pastor and a congregation. I wish to thank the people for their faithful diligence during the twenty years we have been together, their continued willingness to take calculated risks, their graciousness in providing time to write, their help in editing and proofing the manuscript, and most of all, the way they have held me accountable.

A special word of gratitude to Kennon Callahan for the inspiration to begin this work; Wallace Fisher for guidance as I wrote; Lyle Schaller for his continual guidance; Marilynn Wacker, Don Hilkemeier, Vicki Bear, and Gerry Staffel for proofing the manuscript; Beverly Martin and Susan McMahon for patience at the word processor; and Milton Lewis, who at times shouldered more than his share of our ministry.

The information on the churches used as supportive examples of the Twenty Principles was gathered from several sources: *The United Methodist Reporter* in Dallas, Texas; *Parable Churches* by Ralph and Nell Mohney; seminars I've done in local churches during the last three years; and personal interviews with pastors.

In chapters 3, 5, and 6, an asterisk (*) by the name of a church indicates that the information was obtained from the "Church Aflame" series of *The United Methodist Reporter*, which dealt with "United Methodist congregations of all sizes that are growing numerically, shouldering their fair share of the denomination's financial obligations, and providing outstanding ministries in their communities." Much appreciation is expressed to the *Reporter* for material concerning the following churches:

First United Methodist Church, Cleveland, Ohio—
   "$140,000 Ad Drive Aims to Revive Church"
   Susan Carroll Aguren, staff writer—Dec. 26, 1986
Dayspring United Methodist Church, Tempe, Ariz.—
   "Burning Sense of Christian Mission, Community,
     Ignites Growing Church"
   Stephen L. Swecker, associate editor—July 24, 1987
Asbury United Methodist Church, Salisbury, Md.—
   "'Full-service' Philosophy Fosters Growth"
   Susan Carroll Aguren, staff writer—Oct. 9, 1987
El Mesias United Methodist Church, Elgin, Ill.—
   "Recruiting Disciples Helps Church Burst at Seams"
   Stephen L. Swecker, associate editor—Jan. 22, 1988
Lake Magdelena (Fla.) United Methodist Church—
   "Fast-growing Florida UMC Emphasizes 'Faith Stories'"
   Glen Larum, associate editor—April 15, 1988
Aldersgate United Methodist Church, Olathe, Kan.—
   "'Baby Boomer' UMC: Aldersgate Targets Young Families"
   Glen Larum, associate editor—July 8, 1988
Brentwood (Tenn.) United Methodist Church—
   "'Something Going on All the Time' at Brentwood UMC"
   Douglas F. Cannon, associate editor—Aug. 12, 1988
First United Methodist Church, Plymouth, Mich.—
   "Plymouth Church Rocks with Sounds of Happy 'Family'"
   Glen Larum, associate editor—Sept. 16, 1989
University Methodist Church, Syracuse, N. Y.—
   "'Bubble-up Theology' Revives Urban UM Church"
   John A. Lovelace, managing editor—Oct. 14, 1988
Trinity United Methodist Church, Denver, Colo.—
   "Denver's Trinity UMC: New Flames from Dying Embers"
   Rita Healy, freelance writer—Nov. 25, 1988
Ben Hill United Methodist Church, Atlanta, Ga.—
   "Ben Hill 'pays' Attention to the Gospel"
   Denise Johnson Stovall, associate editor—July 7, 1989

A final word is due my wife, who spent many lonely evenings this past year. Though her understanding and patience can never fully be repaid, I *will* find the time to try.

                                  Bill Easum

CHAPTER ONE

The Credentials

ARE YOU INTERESTED IN CHURCH GROWTH PRINCIPLES WITH BIBLICAL INTEGRITY? Does it concern you that mainline Protestantism has been dying for twenty-five years? *(Mainline Protestant* refers to United Methodist, Episcopal, Presbyterian, United Church of Christ, Lutheran, and some Southern Baptist churches.) Are you interested in having a healthy church that nurtures its members and reaches the unchurched? Are you searching for biblical church-growth principles that fit the attitude and climate of mainline Protestant churches today?

There is good news for mainline Protestants. There are biblical growth principles that can reverse our slow but steady death and develop healthy churches.

This book shares twenty proven growth principles drawn from my twenty years' experience as pastor of Colonial Hills United Methodist Church in San Antonio, Texas. During those twenty years, Colonial Hills grew over 600 percent in worship attendance and also developed a balanced ministry that includes evangelism, social action, and missions. Today Colonial Hills is larger than 99.6 percent of all Protestant churches in America.

Lyle Schaller, a consultant for Yokefellow Institute, after a 1984 review of the church's operations, said of Colonial Hills:

> Unquestionably, the most remarkable characteristic of this twenty-four-year-old congregation is that it combines the

three historical strands of American Methodism—evange-lism, social justice, and missions—and at the same time has increased the average attendance at Sunday morning worship more than sevenfold.

The growth principles I am speaking of are not peculiar to Colonial Hills. Hundreds of healthy, growing churches across America intentionally and unintentionally use these principles. And there are many parallels between these twenty principles and the philosophy of the Growth Plus movement of The United Methodist Church.

To highlight the universality of these principles, I have included in this book forty-one concrete examples from thirty growing, healthy churches of varied size, denomination, and ethnic make-up, from seventeen different states. Each of these churches is an excellent example of one or more growth principles.

CAUTION: Do not think that just because a given example comes from a church larger than yours, it isn't applicable to your church. Small churches grew to be large churches by using these principles. They can be applied to any size church.

The Context

Like many churches organized in the two decades following World War II, Colonial Hills did not fulfill the expectations of its sponsors. Constituted in 1960, it grew for six years to more than one hundred present at worship services, and then began to die. When I became the pastor in 1969, fewer than fifty people worshiped on an average Sunday morning.

My first appointment was with the president of the bank that held the mortgage on our property. He was nice but clear. The church must begin paying on the mortgage or face foreclosure!

On sharing this conversation with the congregation, I discovered a small remnant who shared my concern over the decline of the church. For the next six months, as we met almost weekly, we discovered that we were not really interested in our church's survival. Instead, our common vision was to have a growing, healthy church that nurtured its members and also reached the unchurched.

Reasons for Decline

We concluded that our church was dying for four reasons. I am now convinced that most mainline Protestant-ism is dying for the same four reasons:

One, the church was more concerned about its survival as an institution than about meeting the spiritual and physical needs of people.

Two, the importance of worship was misunderstood and downplayed.

Three, many of the church members and our institutional representatives had a bias against church growth.

Four, few members were willing to pay the price of hard work necessary for a church to grow and be healthy.

During the first year we looked for ways to address these four problems. We searched the Scriptures; we conducted numerous house meetings and one-on-one interviews with ex-members and uninvolved neighbors, to determine their perceptions and attitudes about our church; we studied the prevailing conditions of most of the mainline Protestant denominations; and we prayed.

Four Building Blocks

We concluded that four basic building blocks form the vision for growing, healthy, mainline Protestant churches. Chapter 2 will explore the biblical basis for the kind of church growth that can be built upon the foundation provided by these four building blocks:

Building Block One: Ministry must be Christ-centered, to meet the needs of the people, not of the institution. Churches are here to help people, not people to help churches. People-oriented churches tend to grow; denominationally oriented churches tend to die.

Building Block Two: Worship is the initial building block of congregational life, sustained and nurtured by Christian education. Worship is the short-term barometer of a church's health; education is the long-term barometer. People must be fed before they can go out into the world and live a Christian life.

Building Block Three: God wants the church to grow and grow. Churches can grow with integrity. Intentional strategies are necessary in order to reach out into the community with the message of God's love. Lay people need to learn that they are best served when they serve those not yet part of the Christian faith.

Building Block Four: God expects our very best. Growth was easy for mainline Protestants in the 1940s and 1950s, but it isn't now, and all indications are that it will be harder in the future. Thus strategic planning, which blends mainline Protestant theology with good business practices, is essential.

The Law of Congregational Life

One simple law, or Christian dynamic, as trustworthy as a law of physics, undergirds these four building blocks, and it is true of every Christian church. The law is this: Churches, like people, are healthiest when they reach out to others rather than worry about themselves. Churches grow because they intentionally reach out; churches die because they dwell on their own internal problems. The biblical text for this law, Acts 1:8*b*, will be discussed in chapter 2.

Growth Principles

As we applied the four building blocks at Colonial Hills, twenty growth principles emerged. These principles worked every time we applied them, and in every stage of our growth. They have now been tested with more than five hundred churches in forty-four states, and the positive results suggest that they will work in mainline Protestant churches of all sizes.

SECOND CAUTION: The size of your church does not matter. Allow these growth principles to shape your leadership and decision making. Find suitable concrete ways to use them in your church, and it will grow with integrity.

Each principle stands on its own, but all are necessary for biblical church growth. The level of importance of each principle depends upon the condition and location of your church. The following chapters will explain and examine these growth principles as they relate to one of the four building blocks.

The Ministry Audit

As we at Colonial Hills applied the growth principles to real situations, we developed a tool we named the Ministry Audit. This tool (see chapter 7) will provide the framework in which to do your strategic planning for a healthy congregation. It will help you "red flag" your problems as they begin, and it will point out the windows of opportunity early enough so that you can take advantage of them before they pass you by.

After reading the entire book, go through each section of the Ministry Audit and determine whether its use can be of major benefit to your congregation. If the decision is Yes, ask your church to authorize either a standing committee or special task force on strategic planning whose members would read this book and complete the Ministry Audit. This will provide your church with the necessary data from which to do the kind of planning that results in biblical church growth.

CHAPTER TWO

The Basic Law
of Congregational Life

And you shall be my witnesses in Jerusalem and in Judea and Samaria and to the ends of the earth.

Acts 1:8*b*

CHURCHES GROW WHEN THEY INTENTIONALLY REACH OUT TO PEOPLE INSTEAD OF CONCENTRATING ON THEIR INSTITUTIONAL NEEDS; churches die when they concentrate on their own needs. This is the basic Law of Congregational Life.

As a young boy, I was fascinated by the effect of throwing pebbles into a pond. One tiny pebble would produce an ever-widening circle that eventually filled the entire pond, and if I waited long enough, and if I had thrown the stone near the center of the pond, when the ripple reached the bank, it rippled back to the original point of entry.

The church of Jesus Christ is like an ever-widening circle. As it gives itself away on behalf of others, it grows. Everything we do on behalf of others comes back to us. This is the way life works. We give and we receive.

One week after preaching a sermon titled The Ever-widening Circle, I received a note from a member of the church: "It's time for some sermons about personal and spiritual growth as well as institutional growth. We have some needs out here, too!"

The member missed the point of the sermon. Churches are healthiest when they reach out. Members are best nurtured when they nurture others. The art of giving has healing effects. Jesus taught us this in all he said and did: Those who lose their lives will find them (Matt. 10:39). We have a need to help others. God made us that way. We find emotional and spiritual health by moving beyond concern for self.

Let's be very clear. This book is not about growth for growth's sake, but about helping churches reach out to meet the needs of people. In the process of helping others, two things happen: Churches develop physical, mental, and spiritual health; and they grow numerically. Life works this way for both the church and the individual. When this law of congregational life is the basis for ministry, growth with integrity happens.

Figure 1

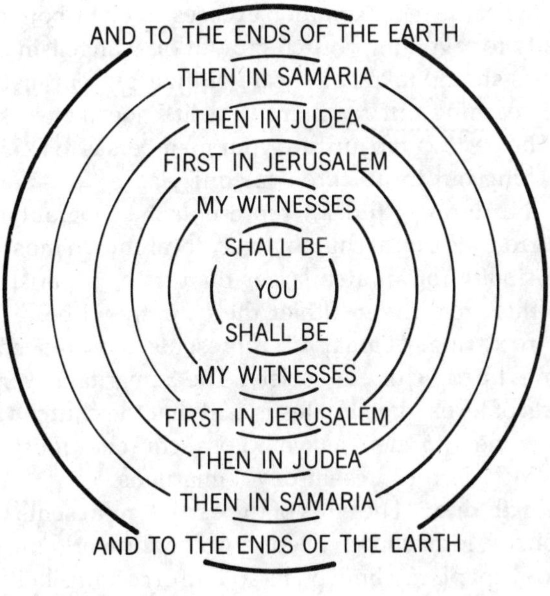

AND TO THE ENDS OF THE EARTH

THEN IN SAMARIA

THEN IN JUDEA

FIRST IN JERUSALEM

MY WITNESSES

SHALL BE

YOU

SHALL BE

MY WITNESSES

FIRST IN JERUSALEM

THEN IN JUDEA

THEN IN SAMARIA

AND TO THE ENDS OF THE EARTH

The Biblical Basis

Although the Bible is filled with references to the Law of Congregational Life, I intend to use only one. Jesus talked about this law in the commission he left with his disciples in the upper room. He instructed them in the law when he said, "You shall be my witnesses in Jerusalem and in all Judea and Samaria and to the end of the earth" (Acts 1:8b). Our Lord's last words are very clear—the mission of the church is to continually increase its ability to give itself away on behalf of all God's creation.

Examine Figure 1. I call this The Ever-widening Circle. The circles represent the life cycle of a church. It is the biblical affirmation that the farther a congregation moves from the center, the healthier the church becomes. The less of "you" and the more of God there is at the center of the circle, the healthier the congregation.

The third ring, "Jerusalem," represents a local congregation. One of the more common excuses given by both clergy and laity for avoiding church growth or evangelism is that churches should take better care of their present members before reaching out for more. But life doesn't work that way. The best way to nurture your members is to join them in reaching out to nurture someone else.

The fourth ring, "Judea," represents the geographic area that surrounds a local church. Every local church must feel a responsibility for an area larger than its own parish. The larger this area, the healthier the church will be.

The next ring, "Samaria," represents the unloved and unwanted people of our society. The Samaritans were the outcasts of Jesus' day, but Jesus said that the church was to be his witness to them as well. Local churches must reach out to include the present-day Samaritans.

The sixth ring, "The ends of the earth," represents world missions. A local church needs a vision for world missions that does not place a limit on its sphere of responsibility. For church growth with integrity, a church must really believe that with God's help, there are no limits to the scope of its ministry. The circle always must be growing wider.

The Argument

The Law of Congregational Life is the basis for biblical ministry because it focuses on life's fundamental challenge: to overcome self-centeredness. Jesus asked us to be his witnesses, not our own. He asked us to move away from considering ourselves the center of our universe, to put other in our place. He knew that when we do so, we become healthy.

One Sunday after worship I received an anonymous note scribbled on the back of a registration card: "Who says our church has to grow? I think Colonial Hills has grown enough." On another occasion when I announced a series on The Ever-widening Circle, I received this note: "Please make it clear at the beginning that growth for growth's sake is not what you're talking about." At another time, I was handed one that read: "I hope we're not trying to reach more new members just to fund the budget."

Among mainline Protestants, church growth is almost as difficult to talk about as money or politics. Why? Probably because we do not want to lose control of our own church; new people mean less control for ourselves. We are comfortable the way we are, and we do not like to change to accommodate new people and new ideas.

The Law of Congregational Life is a reminder that life does not revolve around *self*. As a rule, twentieth-century Christians have not understood that life centers around our relationship with Christ and others, not around ourselves. We have viewed the mission of the church primarily in light of our own personal needs. We have failed to understand that we are made in such a way that our needs are nurtured best as we take care of the needs of others. When we talk about taking care of our own membership before being involved in evangelism or outreach, we reveal a lack of understanding of the mission of the church. The basic mission of the church is to help me nurture others, and in that process, I will be nurtured too!

New Hampshire is one of only three United Methodist conferences north of a line drawn from North Carolina to Arizona that grew in net membership in 1986. I contacted the pastors of two of the growing churches in New Hampshire to ask why their congregations had reversed the decline. The answers they shared could be multiplied hundreds of times across America.

For almost two decades Portsmouth United Methodist Church had steadily declined to an average worship attendance of thirty. Since the arrival of pastor David A. Kerr in 1982, the congregation has grown to an average of two hundred at worship service. There are several reasons for this turnaround, but one stands out: The church intentionally identified needs and reached out to meet those needs! A variety of short-term ministries was offered to the transient population in the town's two military bases. The worship service became an event where people felt loved and wanted. The church emphasized its openness to new people and provided opportunities for fellowship. Realizing that neighborhoods no longer were the primary place where people developed their relationships, the church began a serious advertising campaign in the newspaper and on television and radio. And Portsmouth UMC began to grow because it identified a need and reached out to fill it.

Moultonboro United Methodist Church in New Hampshire has a similar story. As in many New England towns, the people there had a wait-and-see attitude toward newcomers. Under the leadership of two pastors, the church has stopped its decline and grown from a worship attendance of around twenty-five to almost one hundred twenty. The Reverend David E. Svenson gives two reasons for this recovery. First, the church realized that the community was beginning to grow and intentionally planned ministries for the members to "go missional" to reach out beyond the church. Members were constantly made aware of United Methodist Missions abroad; many participated in the short-term Volunteers in Mission program, in which members go to foreign countries for two weeks of service. The church also established the Neighbors in Need program, in which members had one-on-one experiences in helping people outside the church. Second, the people decided not only to welcome newcomers but to share the power with them by giving them responsible positions within the leadership of the church. Any time a congregation intentionally reaches out to help others, it will grow!

Why Do Churches Grow and Die?

Allow me to introduce Joe. Joe has been married for ten years. He and his wife have two children—one six years of age; the other, three months. Neither Joe nor his wife have been to church since they left their parents' homes. The oldest child is now ready to start school, and Joe's wife decides it is also time for the children to receive a Christian education. Joe doesn't want to go to church, but he gives in because his wife insists.

The first obstacle Joe faces is a lack of convenient parking. By the time he gets to the church, he is irritated because he had to walk a block. The second obstacle is the absence of directional signs to the nursery. No member of the church is willing to break away from a personal conversation to help them find their way. By now Joe is fuming.

Finally Joe's family locates the sanctuary, only to sit shoulder-to-shoulder with a lot of strangers. Joe does not like to have strangers that close. He wants plenty of elbow room. As the service progresses, Joe is asked to hold up his hand so that everyone will know he is not a member. He does not want anyone to know he is there, much less that he is not a member.

Then without warning, the whole congregation suddenly rises and begins to sing something that all good Christians are supposed to know—the Doxology. Joe doesn't know the Doxology. The page number is printed in the bulletin, so he frantically finds the right place, only to realize that the song is over.

The sermon puts Joe to sleep because it talks about things he cannot apply to his daily life, and it uses words with which he is not familiar. When the service is over, Joe and his family leave without being greeted by anyone. Later, Joe informs his wife that he does not intend to go through that torture again!

Now allow me to introduce Max. Max is a long-term member of the church Joe just visited. His children are all grown. He is a few years from retirement, and he has helped the church with several building programs. Max has been a member for so long he can't remember what it's like to be uncommitted to Christ and his church.

When told about Joe's reaction to his visit to their church, Max said, "If he isn't any more committed than that, let him stay at home. I don't mind walking a block to church. Besides, he's probably not willing to help pay for a new sanctuary anyway."

Mainline Protestant churches are filled with good people like Max, and because of that, they are dying. Dying churches fail to remember that many of their present members were once just like Joe. They were not committed, and they could have cared less about attending church. Today's world is filled with people like Joe—good people with good families, but unchurched and uncommitted.

There is a world of difference between the value systems of Max and Joe. Max believes people should be as far out of debt as possible; Joe thinks the more credit he has, the more affluent he is. Max trusts institutions; Joe doesn't. Max serves God out of duty, obligation, and commitment; Joe serves out of compassion. Max has long-term plans and goals; Joe prefers instant gratification. Max married for life; Joe married in the hope that it would last. Max grew up in church; Joe did not. For growth to occur in mainline Protestant churches, Max must recognize the difference between his world and Joe's world.

Mainline Protestant churches will once again be a vital

force in society if they address the needs of Joe's new world, instead of trying to preserve their old traditions. Growing churches are filled with Maxes who are willing to make it possible for Joe to hear the gospel and be loved by the people long enough for Christian growth to begin.

Integrity Factors

Because there is always the danger that numbers and quantity can take precedence over a concern for people, any discussion about church growth *must* include enough integrity factors to avoid the possibility that quantity will become the primary emphasis of ministry. There are at least seven integrity factors present in healthy church growth:

1. People take precedence over institutional maintenance.
2. Ministry must be balanced.
3. There is a high ratio between the membership and the number of people who attend worship.
4. There is a balance between money spent on the church and money spent on others.
5. A higher percentage of members join by profession of faith and restoration of vows than by transfer of membership.
6. Growth is stable and steady.
7. An inclusive faith is stressed.

These seven factors will be examined in various places throughout this book.

Summary

The Law of Congregational Life is that churches are healthiest when they reach out to others. Churches grow because they are intentionally concerned about the needs of others. Churches die because they concentrate primarily on their internal needs. With this law before us, we are now ready to explore the growth principles.

CHAPTER THREE

A People-centered Ministry

While there is an intense search for spiritual moorings, churches in many instances appear unprepared to answer these spiritual needs.

Emerging Trends,
Princeton Religion Research Center, 1980

GROWING CHURCHES ARE MORE CONCERNED WITH PEOPLE THAN WITH THE PRESERVATION OF INSTITUTIONS. The religious leaders of Jesus' day made people feel that they existed to serve their religion. Throughout his ministry Jesus challenged those leaders on this flaw in their ministry. He always addressed people's needs; he made them feel that their religion existed to serve their needs. He said that the object of religion was people, not the observance of the Law.

Avoid telling your members that the church needs them. The church doesn't need people—people need the church. Churches feel they need people only because churches don't meet the needs of people.

Ask one key question of all new members and first-time visitors: "Tell us what you need, and if we don't have it, we'll help you get it started." From their answers, develop your programs and discover your leaders. Make sure that 10 percent of your budget goes to provide a variety of program opportunities, including training, to nurture the members of the congregation.

Growth Principles

Growth Principle One: Growth is Not Concerned with Numbers, But with Meeting the Needs of People.

People are the church's only asset, its only profit margin, and its only bottom line. Programs are merely the vehicles through which people minister to one another. Denominational programs should be used only if they meet the grass-roots needs of the churched and the unchurched.

Find a need and fill it. Within three years, Wesley United Methodist Church in Harlingen, Texas, ended a two-decade membership decline of 30 percent. Located in the Rio Grande Valley, Harlingen is 85 percent Hispanic; has a population of 50,000, which includes large numbers of winter tourists; and has a fragile economy, due to the vulnerability of the citrus industry and the area's close ties to the Mexican peso.

When Robert Schnase became the pastor in 1984, worship attendance averaged 184, and the church struggled financially, unable to pay its apportionments while trying to maintain its facilities. Since that time Wesley has grown 53 percent in worship, 22 percent in Sunday school, 49 percent in budget, 54 percent in income, and 82 percent in mission giving; attendance and income continue to rise 10 percent annually.

One of the main reasons cited for this reversal is the church's willingness to develop new programs to reach out into the community. One such program, designed to meet the needs of young adults, is Parents' Night Out. Once a month, quality child care is offered free on Friday evening to allow parents to enjoy an evening out, while their children are cared for in a loving Christian atmosphere. Average attendance is fifty. As a result of this and other innovative programs, the number of young adults in the church has quadrupled; 45 percent of new members joined in 1987 by confession of faith; and the weekday preschool has increased by 52 percent.

Since 1981, a baby-boomer church, Aldersgate United Methodist Church in Olathe, Kansas,* has grown in worship attendance from 138 to 320. According to pastor Ira DeSpain, the reason for the growth is the congregation's decision to intentionally meet the needs of young adults. Fifty-one percent of the membership is under junior-high age; 25 percent of the adult membership was baptized at Aldersgate; only one-third of the new members joined by United Methodist transfer.

One of the most needed specialized ministries in every part of the nation is a ministry to singles. Before starting such a ministry, you need to know several things: No other program will ebb and flow, depending on staff involvement, as much as a singles ministry; two singles will give as much financially as one couple; the counseling load will increase; if using lay volunteers, singles ministries are best started by a couple; by the time the program has an average attendance of more than fifty, a quarter- to half-time paid staff person is helpful; singles programs work best if Sunday morning classes are divided into two or three age groups, with all the groups meeting together at some point during the week; singles will drive anywhere in town for an active program; and they return primarily because of the enthusiasm of the group—the larger and more varied the activities, the better.

Located near the University of Washington, University Presbyterian Church in Seattle averages more than four hundred singles each Sunday in two singles classes, divided at age thirty-two. On Tuesday evening the two groups meet for a meal, Bible studies, support groups, and organizational meeting. A full-time staff person oversees the numerous activities, both social and religious.

In order to develop programs that address the needs expressed by the people, it is helpful if a pastor

understands the everyday world of the members. Understanding of people must not be limited to what is read or
perceived through counseling or what is learned at church.
Such knowledge is incomplete. It is helpful if a pastor has
made a living in some way other than the ministry and has
paid rent or made mortgage payments. Such experiences
help pastors understand the needs of the laity.

*Monitor yearly the age, sex, and marital status of the
congregation.* Once a year, take a survey during worship for
four consecutive weeks (see Appendix, Chart 1). If more
than 60 percent of a worshiping congregation is female,
stress male-oriented opportunities. If more than 35 percent
of a congregation is over 50, concentrate on opportunities
for families with children at home. If less than 20 percent of
a congregation consists of divorced singles, consider the
possibilities of a singles ministry.

Next, call the Chamber of Commerce to get the age, sex,
and marital makeup of your general area. Compare these
figures with the survey from your worship services and
respond to those areas in which there are wide differences.
For example, if 53 percent of the worshiping congregation is
over 50, and only 22 percent of the population is over 50,
your church is considerably older than the area. If only 20
percent of the worshiping congregation is between 21 and
34, while 35 percent of the population is between 21 and 34,
your church needs to concentrate on reaching young
adults.

*The size of the congregation determines the method of discovering
individual needs.* Churches with an average worship attendance of fewer than two hundred may want to concentrate on
the one-to-one approach, with the pastor relating to each
individual. Churches with worship attendance from two to
five hundred may find it best to concentrate on programs that
speak to personal needs and involve either the pastor or a
staff member who is in close contact with a large segment of
the congregation. Churches with a worship attendance of

more than five hundred will want to develop as many small groups as possible; here the laity can begin to take serious pastoral roles among the congregation.

Deal openly with controversy. Controversy plus confrontation (and/or dialogue) equals growth. When people are forced to confront their differences in the Christian arena, growth occurs. Some will drop out, but those who stay will grow in their understanding of people and in their ability to defend what they believe.

Much of what goes on at church meetings is therapy. People bring to these meetings the pressures and anxieties of their daily life. Some simply need a way to vent their frustrations. For others, it may be the only place they can exercise any authority. High-powered business people are less likely to drop out of leadership if they understand the need some members have for this kind of therapy.

Consider the psychological needs of members of boards or committees. If your basic decision-making board consists of twenty-five or more members, it is too unwieldy to do much more than receive information and vote Yes, No, or Wait. These are information boards. Members of this size board who expect to have serious input or debate concerning the direction of the church soon begin to feel that the board is nothing more than a rubber stamp for someone else's programs. If you want a "working board" where decisions are hammered out, keep the membership under twenty-five. If you wish to use the board as a point of information and for giving approval or disapproval to already thoroughly formulated ideas, the number of members does not matter. What does matter is that the members of the board know the rules and what is expected of them.

If your board has more than twenty-five members, there is a need for an executive committee of no more than ten key elected officials to do the basic work in preparation for the board meetings. All items to be voted on by the board should come through this committee. The larger the church, the more important it is to have a small executive committee and a large board.

Make sure that the blessing of new ideas is stronger than the withholding of permission. Every congregation has those few who do not represent the majority, but who wish to withhold permission from an action with which they do not agree. Even when the vast majority of the members are ready to start a new ministry, it is always easier to stop a new idea than to give permission.

The larger the church, the more important it is that members feel free to give permission to new ventures in which they have no intention of participating. Often members feel they should base their vote on whether they intend to participate in a venture. You've probably heard some well-intentioned leader say, "Don't vote for this issue unless you intend to support it with your dollars." The giving and withholding of permission should not be dependent solely upon one's participation in the venture. An understanding of this principle will free elderly members whose only income may be from Social Security to vote positively on issues they agree with, even though they cannot participate financially.

A church that cares about people cultivates a positive image within the community. Churched and unchurched people talk about your church. One way to find out what is being said is to ask the receptionist what most people call the church to ask about. Once you know what they are saying, build on the good that is being said or change the negative image. More people attend, or don't attend, your church because of what is said on the community grapevine.

Growth Principle Two: Growth Occurs When People Are Given a Wide Variety of Choices.

The homogeneous principle of church growth, which teaches that churches grow by reaching out to like-minded people, has destroyed much of the integrity of church growth. It does not reflect the diversity of biblical faith or the richness of American culture.

The earliest attempt to promote a form of homogeneous church growth occurred at the Jerusalem Conference, recorded in the fifteenth chapter of Acts. Paul and Barnabas were called before the elders for questioning because they were allowing Gentiles into the faith without first requiring circumcision. The Jerusalem church wanted to impose their own experience and expression of faith on all converts. Soon that church was dying and had to rely on the newly established churches for support. By contrast, Paul continued to allow Gentiles to become Christians without circumcision, and the churches he established withstood the test of time.

Churches need to expand in ways that encourage every aspect of biblical faith to grow and be appreciated within the congregation. Rather than seeking conformity, churches need to draw upon the richness of their diversity. As John Wesley said, "In the essentials—unity; in the nonessentials—freedom; in all things—love."

All white, 145-year-old Ryland Epworth United Methodist Church in southeast Washington, D. C., reversed the gradual decline experienced by so many older small and middle-sized churches by becoming more diverse and heterogeneous. Over the last ten years, 25 percent of the new members have been black. The average attendance at worship has steadily increased, many young adults have joined, the income and budget have doubled, additional staff has been added, and mission obligations have been met.

Andrew Meeder, pastor of Ryland Epworth, cites two strategies that helped the church emphasize its diversity. First, it established an Administrative Council which involves both new and long-term members in the decision-making process. Every other month, the council functions as a working/planning session, with no need to make immediate decisions. The next month, the council meets in "executive session," during which actual decisions are made. The makeup between new and long-term members is almost 50-50.

Second, each Sunday of the month there is a different form of worship in order to offer theological, missional, musical, and liturgical diversity. On the first Sunday, Holy Communion is celebrated in a variety of ways. The second Sunday reflects a traditional service. On the third Sunday, there is no printed bulletin, and the service is informal and evangelistic. The fourth Sunday emphasizes the social dimension of the gospel, since faith without works is dead. On the fifth Sunday, anything can happen.

Once a neighborhood church, Ryland Epworth now draws people from as far as twenty miles away. It is a reminder to older mainline Protestant churches that if they are open to diversity, the best is yet to come.

Intentionally establish and promote a balanced ministry. Divide your ministry into three categories—*love, justice,* and *mercy* (see Figure 2). The ministry of *love* nurtures those who are following Christ. The roles are pastoral. The objectives are aimed at developing solid relationships between the members themselves and between the members and God. Shepherding ministries are part of this area of the church's life.

The ministry of *justice* agitates God's people into taking action against the root causes of injustice. The roles are prophetic. The object is to involve church members in the public arena, and controversy is an inevitable part of this ministry.

The ministry of *mercy* focuses on reconciling people to themselves, to others, and to God. The roles are evangelical. The object is to provide an arena such as worship and evangelism, so that people are touched with God's forgiveness to the point that their lives are changed.

Asbury United Methodist Church in Salisbury, Maryland,* describes itself as a "full service" church. The facilities are open to the community seven days a week. The church seeks ways to serve people rather than trying to gain

members. As a result, there is a lot of goodwill toward the
church, as seen in the fact that vandalism of church
property has declined. Using this "full service" slogan,
Asbury has turned around a twenty-year decline and added
some two hundred fifty members in the last six years.
Founded in 1798, Asbury's membership peaked in 1962 at
1,506, but slipped to 1,313 in 1977. Today there are 1,620
members. Worship attendance averaged 348 in 1977 and
has grown to 410 in 1988.

Figure 2: A Balanced Ministry

LOVE	JUSTICE	MERCY
Nurture	Agitation	Reconciliation
Pastoral	Prophetic	Evangelical
One to One	Public Arena	Worship

*A balanced ministry in the 1990s will include quality child care:
preschool, kindergarten, mothers' day out, day care, summer
camps.* Six of the fastest growing United Methodist churches
studied in *Parable Churches* by Ralph and Nell Mohney
(Nashville: Discipleship Resources, 1989) list quality child
care as one of their main ministries. Consider these points
when establishing or running weekday programs for
children:

1. Weekday preschool, kindergarten, mothers' day out,
and day care should be part of the educational and outreach
ministries of your church, not run as separate entities.

2. The directors of these programs are considered staff
and meet weekly with other staff or pastor.

3. Every parent who enrolls in the weekday program
should be considered a potential new member and should
be added to your mailing list for both programs and
stewardship.

4. The preschool and mothers' day out should be not
only self-supporting but should also contribute at least 15

percent of their income to the general budget of the church, unless providing scholarships for the needy is part of the church's mission.

5. Rooms used by the preschool and mothers' day out should not dictate to the Sunday school how it can use the rooms on Sunday morning. Make sure that as much equipment and as many supplies as possible are interchangeable and shared.

Provide a choice in the hours for Sunday morning worship. Whether or not your space dictates the need for a second or third worship service, consider providing a choice. When Colonial Hills moved into its fourth sanctuary in 1980, the third morning worship service was continued, even though we had plenty of space without it. When possible, regularly offer a choice of preachers on Sunday morning. Colonial Hills has offered a choice of two preachers for the past ten years. Many members now attend services based upon who is preaching.

CAUTION: Once an additional service of worship is begun, do your best never to drop it. People go to that service because they prefer the hour, or the people, or the music, or the preacher. When a service of worship is discontinued, it is not unusual for up to 20 percent of those worshiping at that service to drop out.

Every three to six months, start a new adult Sunday school class built around content or relationships or a personality, rather than on age or sex. First United Methodist Church in the small, stable town of Temple, Texas, had an average Sunday school attendance of just over 400, including twelve adult classes divided along age lines, none of which could have been described as a Bible study class or a singles class. On January 1, 1989, the church organized both a Bible study class and a singles class, and Sunday school attendance increased by 37 people within two months. Of those attending these two classes, only one couple was already active in Sunday school.

After six months of existence, Sunday school classes will draw mainly from new members; they seldom attract people from within the present membership, who have decided they do not like either the content, the leader, the people in the class, or the time or place the class is offered.

A well-rounded adult Sunday school program will reflect the makeup of both the congregation and the community, and consist of both discussion and lecture, as well as provide diverse opportunities for subject content.

Growth Principle Three: Growth Occurs When People Are Matched with Their Skills.

Don't try to fit volunteers into the needs of the church. Instead, determine the skills of the volunteers and provide opportunities for those skills to be used.

Frazer Memorial United Methodist Church has one of the largest volunteer programs in mainline Protestantism. Each year 3,500 lay people volunteer in one of the 150 ministries offered in brochure form, ranging from office work to parking-lot traffic control. An amazing 82 percent of the membership serves in some area of the church.

Located in Montgomery, Alabama, and pastored by John Ed Mathison, Frazer is the fastest growing church in United Methodism—from 609 members in 1972 to 4,800 in 1986. Every Sunday 3,000 worship, making this also the largest worshiping church. Only 15 percent of the members have missed worship during the last six weeks.

The secret of that success is that the church concentrates on getting people involved in something that meets their needs, rather than just asking them to join the church. Frazer works on the belief that people are not interested in maintaining a system, but that they do care deeply about meeting the needs of other people.

Tailor the nominating process to fit the ministry and makeup of the congregation. Develop a set of leadership positions that reflect the objectives of your congregation. Provide job descriptions for each position and nominate people to those positions. Do not nominate people to positions for which there is no definite mission. Tell prospective leaders that the job description contains the minimal requirements for the position. If the person wishes to do more, fine. But fulfilling the minimal requirements is a must.

Choose those people responsible for programs carefully. The nominating process at Colonial Hills is by invitation only. When we were smaller, our nominating committee met to discuss who it would like to see chair each of the next year's programs. We then sent those people a mission statement outlining what was expected. The people were contacted to see what questions they had and were told that training would be provided if they accepted the invitation. Blanket appeals for people to serve have not been made at Colonial Hills since the mid-1970s.

Churches with more than five hundred who attend worship services will find the following procedures helpful. Ask each staff person and member of the nominating committee to provide a list of twenty-five mainly new members they feel have potential for leadership. Invite the people who appear on two or more of the lists to attend a dessert party at a member's home. In the invitation, tell them their names have been submitted by members of the staff and nominating committee and that only a certain number of people have been invited. Also tell them that several important leadership positions will be offered to them that night.

Colonial Hills has had excellent results with this process. Most of our primary leadership positions are filled that night, and new leaders are discovered. A variety of people are deployed, and the staff has direct input in the nominating process.

Growth Principle Four: Growth Does Not Dictate That More People Will Become Inactive.

People do not become inactive just because a church is growing. The drop-out percentage rate for Colonial Hills is no larger now than it was when we were a small church. The national average drop-out rate for a church our size is 10 to 15 percent annually. For the past five years, our drop-out rate has been between 6 and 7 percent.

Concentrate on assimilating new members into the church within the first three months. New members who are quickly assimilated into an area of church life other than worship are 75 percent more likely to be members a year later than those who join and simply attend worship. Review each new member carefully during the first three months to determine what course of action is required to help them belong. New members need to be given immediate access to the inner life of the church so that they can make significant contributions.

There are four immediate points of entry for new members: volunteer work in the office; responsibility for some short-term task for which there is recognition; membership in a small group such as a Sunday school class with fewer than forty people in regular attendance; and participation in a choir.

We use the following ten-step program designed to assimilate every new member into either a role, a task, or a group, in addition to attendance at worship. These steps are not necessarily in order of time. It is best if a paid staff person is responsible for assimilation, since few laity have the twenty to thirty hours required for weekly, intentional assimilation.

STEP ONE: Picture taken, information form and orientation packet given on the Sunday new member joins.

STEP TWO: First Week
a. "Opportunities for Service" brochure and new member pledge card mailed separately.
b. Staff reviews new member names and pictures at staff meeting.

STEP THREE: Second Week
a. Follow up on "Opportunities" brochure.
b. Information passed on to staff members who make the appropriate response or invitation.

STEP FOUR: Worship attendance tracked, with appropriate calls or visits made by Nurture
and Care committee.

STEP FIVE: Follow-up stewardship calls every month
to new members who have not sent in
pledges.

STEP SIX: Invitation to attend the orientation class.

STEP SEVEN: Invited to new member party.

STEP EIGHT: Staff review of all new members in late
summer for identification of potential
leaders, who will then be invited to
leadership party in the fall.

STEP NINE: Annual new member dinner in No-
vember.

STEP TEN: Invitation to newly formed classes or
groups.

Small groups are essential to a low drop-out rate. In a mobile society, most people do not feel they belong until they become part of some small group within the church. A small group consists of fewer than forty people who meet at least once a month for an agreed-upon purpose. Five to seven people seems to be the best size. Whenever the group exceeds seventeen members it is easy for people to be absent and not missed, and it is difficult for everyone to contribute to the conversation.

One small group for every ten persons in attendance at worship is a worthy goal. The larger the church, the more intentional it must be to form new small groups. Once a small group has been in effect for six months, it has attracted all the present church members it will attract. The only potential for growth lies in new members.

Homogeneity is provided in small groups. People tend to gravitate toward people of like mind, so the wider the diversity of programming and people in a church, the more important small groups become. In these groups people learn about themselves by interacting with people of like mind. They are then ready to go out into the diverse atmosphere of the congregation and stand toe to toe with those of differing viewpoints.

In most churches the people who exercise power are those who take time to build up the relationships that result within small groups. They achieve credibility by relating to other people. The trust built up over the years in small-group relationships allows significant corporate decisions to be hammered out by a diverse congregation.

Bruce Larson has served as senior pastor of University Presbyterian Church in Seattle, Washington, since 1982. This seventy-five-year-old church, located near the University of Washington, has an average attendance in worship of 3,300 and a membership of 3,500. University is well known for its emphasis on small groups. More than four hundred small groups meet weekly. The overall emphasis is supervised by a paid staff member who offers suggestions and provides special courses each year on small-group leadership, but each group is free to develop in its own way. Classes are formed around needs that surface from one or more members or visitors. The content of each group varies, but many groups are involved in Bible study. New small groups are formed several times throughout the year.

Members who have been inactive for six months to a year are seldom reactivated. In two instances, a church should definitely concentrate on its inactives: (1) upon the arrival of a new pastor; (2) in rural areas where inactives are the main potential for growth. Inactive members are good potential members for another church, but seldom for the church to which they belonged, unless that church is willing to make inactives a priority. Inactives may become active after some kind of tragedy in the family or after many hours of counseling and/or friendship by a member of the church. In chapter 4 we will discuss the importance of tracking the worship attendance.

The best material available on working with inactives is offered by John Savage of Lead Consultants, Inc., Box 664, Reynoldsburg, OH 43068. The material is offered in two parts, totaling approximately ninety hours of class time. Dr. Savage suggests that if his method is used with care and patience, 30 to 70 percent of all inactives can be brought back into active membership.

Growth Principle Five: Growth Provides a Wider Outreach to People in Need.

"I'm more interested in people than I am in bricks and mortar." "Why can't we spend our money helping people instead of building more buildings?" The average person in the pew does not understand that there is a direct correlation between church growth and the ability to help people outside the church. If your church wants to do more for missions or social programs, it should be concerned about increasing the number of people at worship. The more people at worship, the more money is available for outreach. This principle can hold true even when churches incur a large indebtedness during building programs.

As a rule, growing churches are more open to and passionate about outreach ministries. Almost all the churches used to support the twenty growth principles show a marked increase in their giving to outreach causes. Colonial Hills' giving to missions increased from less than $1,000 in 1969 to over $120,000 in 1986. Our leaders measure much of our progress based on how much we are giving to missions. A minimum dollar goal for churches interested in outreach to people in need is 15 percent of the total income.

Growth Principle Six: Growth Need Not Be Hampered by
Participation in the Public Arena.

According to a report on the unchurched in America by
the Princeton Religion Research Center, 13 percent of
unchurched Americans are interested in involvement in
public issues. Churches involved in the public arena do
attract members, even though they may alienate some.

There can't be much integrity in our growth if we avoid
the social-justice issue. To just give Band-aid help of food
and clothing, no matter how much such things are needed,
is to avoid the heart of the problem. As long as God's people
do not organize around their value system, organized
money will make most of the decisions in this country. It is
Polyannaish to think that our responsibilities in the public
arena end with the voting booth or that religion and politics
don't mix.

St. James United Methodist Church is located in a
fashionable area of Little Rock, Arkansas, where 85 percent
of the homes are worth between $200,000 and $1,000,000.
Under the leadership of John Miles since 1976, the church
has been actively involved in the public arena and has
grown from 240 in worship to between 1,200 and 1,300.

Known in the community as the Church of the Second
Chance, St. James helped establish Planned Parenthood in
Arkansas; fought for the ERA; stood against the Moral
Majority when the teaching of creation science in the public
schools was passed; struggled for justice for African
Americans and women; operates Stone Soup, which helps
feed transients; was one of the founders of Our House,
which shelters and finds jobs for the homeless; is helping
build a home for the elderly; conducts an ongoing program
of sex education for children and youth; participates in an
active prison ministry and has fought for family visitation
programs in the state prison system. St. James actively
pushes for social justice and, at the same time, continues to
be the tenth-fastest-growing United Methodist Church.

Few churches in America, however, have made as large a commitment to attacking the root causes of social injustice as has Colonial Hills. An example of the depth and intensity of our involvement is our relationship with the Industrial Areas Foundation and the Metropolitan Congregational Alliance.

In 1979, Colonial Hills was part of a committee that began to organize Protestant, Catholic, Jewish, and Unitarian congregations across San Antonio. The purpose of our efforts was to train leaders who could publicly articulate their Judeo-Christian values and hold the public officials accountable. Our group hired the New York-based Industrial Areas Foundation (IAF), founded by Saul D. Alinsky, to be our consultant in the organizing process. San Antonio had previous experience with the IAF in the early 1970s when it helped to found Communities Organized for Public Service (COPS), a group of predominately Catholic Hispanics who live on the west side of the city in one of the poorest sections. Because of its radical tactics and its audacity in questioning the power of the Anglo city fathers, COPS was a dirty word with most of our congregation. There was much opposition from the power brokers who did not want to lose control, and many members of Colonial Hills were nervous about mixing religion and politics.

One afternoon when a group of the sponsoring ministers met at Colonial Hills, our guests included the state organizer for the IAF and founder of COPS, Ernesto Cortez, and Father Albert Benevidos, the most powerful Catholic priest in the COPS organization. Both men were disliked by many members of our church.

The meeting had just begun when the city councilman for our district walked in uninvited and demanded to sit in on our "communist" meeting. Mr. Cortez challenged the appropriateness of the councilman's presence so forcefully that he left. By this time, several reporters had arrived and were insisting on information about the "secret communist meeting" being held in our church. Since I was the pastor, I gave a statement.

The evening television news opened with this statement: "A secret meeting of Northside COPS was held at the Colonial Hills United Methodist Church. Ernie Cortez and Father Al Benevidos of COPS were present." The front page of the morning paper listed the names of the pastors and churches involved in the sponsoring committee and asked if the city was ready for a Northside COPS.

But our church weathered that storm and continued to grow. One year and two hundred one-on-one meetings later, Colonial Hills became a charter member of the Metropolitan Congregational Alliance by an almost unanimous vote of the administrative board.

Few of the injustices of this world can be addressed by the church without entering the political arena. Pastors need the freedom to become involved in social justice beyond the pulpit. To simply preach on injustice makes the pastor feel good but accomplishes little. Give your pastor the freedom not only to preach on social justice but also to lead the church into the public arena to hold public officials acountable.

Conclusion

Churches that look for ways to meet the needs of people will automatically grow. Churches that serve only the denomination or institution will die. That's the way life works.

CHAPTER FOUR

Worship— The Number-one Building Block of Congregational Life

> *Go out to the highways and hedges, and compel people to come in, that my house may be filled.*
>
> —Luke 14:23

GROWING CHURCHES HAVE DYNAMIC CORPORATE WORSHIP. The main key to the morale of the congregation, as well as the place where most significant corporate dynamics take place, is Sunday morning worship. Sunday school is not the primary point of entry to the church for most mainline Protestants. With the exception of singles and parents with young children, the vast majority of people attend worship before any other church activity.

The following formula is helpful in understanding the importance of worship and Sunday school: Worship attendance is the barometer for the short-term health of a church because it yields immediate results; Sunday school participation is the barometer for the long-term health, because changes due to education usually take at least two years. If a congregation is in trouble or is dying, the place to initiate change is in worship. Once solid worship is in place, work can begin on the long-term health of the church by giving new life to the Sunday school. Contrary to popular belief, Sunday school growth or decline tends to be driven by the growth or decline of worship (see Chart 2 in the Appendix).

43

Worship attendance is a better way than membership to measure the size of a church. Dying denominations emphasize membership; growing denominations emphasize the average attendance at worship. Membership emphasizes only the institutional aspect of faith; attendance emphasizes faith's personal aspect.

Growth Principles

Growth Principle Seven: Growth Will Occur When Worship Is Intentionally Emphasized.

Joe Harding served for seventeen years as senior pastor of Central United Protestant Church in Richland, Washington, a *declining* community of 30,000. During his ministry, Central Church doubled in worship attendance, from 500 to 1,100. One of the key reasons for this remarkable growth was the emphasis on worship. Each year there was an annual worship crusade.[†] According to Dr. Harding,

> The annual attendance crusade is the most effective way to reclaim inactives and to deepen the commitment of the occasional attender. When people establish a pattern of regular attendance, that pattern continues and always influences others. As attendance grows, social concerns and mission commitments deepen.

Hoosier Memorial United Methodist Church has grown from a new church to almost one thousand members in six years by stressing the worship experience as the heart of the church. This church is not afraid of lively worship and inspiring music. Located in southwest Atlanta, Georgia, in the former Audubon Forest United Methodist Church, a $2.5 million plant disbanded by an all-white congregation, Hoosier Memorial is in an excellent location to attract young

---

[†]A copy of Dr. Harding's "Worship Attendance Crusade Guide" is available through Discipleship Resources, Box 189, Nashville, TN 37202.

black professionals in their thirties and forties who do not want to drive downtown.

Preaching is the central element of worship. Today the average visitor comes to church to hear a sermon, not to participate in corporate worship. In most traditions, a sermon no less than fifteen and no more than twenty minutes in length should be part of worship fifty times a year. In longer than usual services, place the sermon toward the beginning of the service and the special event toward the end. The larger the church, the more important it is for the senior pastor to be in the pulpit at least forty-four Sundays a year.

The best advice for preaching is to "preach from the gut, not from the can." No one wants to hear a canned sermon someone else wrote. Fill the sermon with illustrations from personal experiences and observations rather than illustrations found in books. Let the members see how you have assimilated faith into your own life. Let them hurt when you hurt and hope when you hope.

Never preach the same sermon twice unless the congregation asks you to do so. If a sermon is timely and centered on daily events, it will be too familiar to repeat. And when you move to another church, don't preach the same sermons over again. If new, vital, personal illustrations are not available, don't use a sermon until it is born out of your own experience and your work among the people of the new congregation or community.

A good sermon causes the congregation to experience the biblical event that forms the basis for the sermon; forces the individuals to think; contains primarily one central thought; and builds to a commitment on the part of each member of the congregation.

Pick out ten or twelve people scattered throughout the congregation and preach to them, not to the congregation. Look at each one long enough to be sure you have established contact. Don't read your sermon or rely heavily on notes. Keep the content simple and uncomplicated, and preach for a decision.

The preaching content must be biblically rooted, theologically honest, and relevant. Any recovery among mainline Protestants will include a rediscovery of the art of preaching—preaching that is biblical and relevant to everyday living. Stress the basics—grace, sin, repentance, salvation, justice, ethics, and accountability—found in both Old and New Testament. Avoid using technical terms that need elaborate explanations. Make sure that what you say on Sunday can be applied on Monday at work.

The Lutheran Church of the Holy Trinity in Lancaster, Pennsylvania, is the oldest church in the oldest inland city in the United States. When Wallace Fisher became pastor in 1952, this center-city church contained a dying congregation exclusive in membership, was without a mission in the twentieth century, and was viewed in the community as a bulwark against change and progress. Dr. Fisher determined that the integrity of his ministry would be rooted in his fidelity to the Word of God. This, he judged, would be in the best interest of the congregation.

Not only did Dr. Fisher make the pulpit central to the rebirth of Trinity Church, but his sermons challenged people to think about the world in the light of God's prophetic Word. Some were concerned that he was preaching on matters they thought were none of the church's business—like politics. This running dialogue between pulpit and pew led to regular meetings—Coffee and Conversation with the Clergy. At these gatherings, pastor and congregation together learned to define *how* they would carry out prophetic ministry in the world.

Dr. Fisher's 1954 sermon on McCarthyism set the stage for Trinity Church's development of a long and solid future through the power of the pulpit to speak relevantly to sociopolitical issues. Clergy and laity learned to bring the Word of God to bear on all aspects of human existence. From that time forward, major issues were confronted in the pulpit, discussed openly in the congregation, and acted upon. (See Wallace Fisher, *From Tradition to Mission* [Abingdon Press, 1965])

And the church grew from a few hundred to an average attendance of 1,200 in worship each Sunday, and continued at that level during Dr. Fisher's thirty-year ministry. A Word-centered, culturally relevant pulpit is a must for church growth and effective witness in society.

Next to the sermon, music is the most important part of worship. It is not unusual, with a large choir, for music to comprise up to 40 percent of the worship service. When it does, it provides a way to inspire, motivate, and move the congregation; an immediate place for new members to plug into the life of the congregation; a congregation that is more adequately prepared to receive the sermon; a larger core of regular attenders, since the families and friends of the choir members are more likely to attend regularly; and a good sermon becomes an excellent sermon.

Two things must be present for music to play such a role in worship:

1. Select music that is pleasing to the congregation without sacrificing quality. Musicians tend to select music that is too difficult and too classical for the average person to enjoy. As a rule of thumb, select three musical pieces that are congregational pleasers for every piece that is difficult or unfamiliar. Keep in mind that fewer people listen to classical music than to any other form of music, and the harder the music, the more difficult it is for the average member to be able to sing in the choir. Concentrate on providing a wide variety of music.

2. The ideal choir size is one choir member for every ten people in the pew. If the service averages three hundred, the choir should average thirty. This ratio is one of the most important and most often overlooked statistics evaluated by a pastor.

Prepare the worship bulletin with Joe in mind. Joe's first impressions are formed by the events of worship, so plan the worship service to meet the needs of both Joe and Max. Max values ritual; Joe could care less. Max understands the secret language of the congregation; Joe barely remembers the name of the church. Max is willing to sit through a long service; Joe has other things to do. Max has friends sitting all around him; Joe doesn't know a soul. Max wants to hear all about the potluck supper last week; Joe is more concerned about getting to the golf course. Max doesn't mind a sermon on money; Joe considers it an invasion of privacy. Max wants to hear a sermon on the meaning of prayer; Joe wants to know why God allowed his friend's young son to die.

Joe doesn't know by memory such elements as the Lord's Prayer, the Doxology, or the Gloria Patri, so print them in full in the bulletin. Designate a large, regular place in your bulletin to give visitors a brief insight into your church and how to go about joining. Point out this information during the service, to let visitors know you anticipated their arrival and that people join your church on a regular 'basis. Don't cut corners in preparing or printing the bulletin; it is the first printed material most visitors see, as well as the most widely and thoroughly read. When possible, have it typeset and printed, rather than typed and mimeographed. The expense is no longer prohibitive, since desktop publishing and laser printers allow most churches to typeset their own material at a very nominal cost.

Offer an invitation to join at every service, and allow adequate time for new members to be introduced. Let people join even on Christmas Eve! Allow at least seven minutes for people to join and be introduced; in many traditions, if the service runs longer than an hour, people tend not to join. During the service, spell out the specific ways your congregation accepts new members.

Keep track of worship attendance patterns. Members should be monitored monthly until patterns are established. When those patterns are broken by either stopping or returning, contact should be made by phone or letter. It is important that members be made aware that their absence or return is noticed and that someone cares enough to respond. Contact should be made in a way that the members do not feel scolded for not attending. With the advent of the computer and its relatively low price, any church can keep track of attendance.

Figure 3

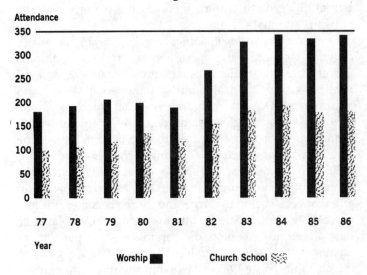

Periodically, analyze the growth patterns of worship. An analysis of the worship pattern over a ten- or twenty-year period will help a congregation in strategic planning.

Consider the growth pattern shown in Figure 3. The key years are 1979, 1982, and 1984. An analysis of the church represented in this graph revealed what happened in these years. The sanctuary could hold an average of 216. (In chapter 5, I will discuss how to arrive at this figure.) The average attendance at worship in 1979 was 208. In 1982 the average attendance jumped to 256 because they started a second service. In 1984 the growth pattern stopped and began to decline because the 11:00 service again reached the magic level of 216. Until this church adds more space, worship attendance will continue to grow for awhile, then begin to decline. Over the years, it will repeat this pattern.

An analysis of this church's growth pattern shows that it needs to do one of two things to stop going up and down. It needs to either provide more seating in worship or start a third service. The analysis also gives added support to the belief that the immediate health of the congregation is driven by worship, not Sunday school. The Sunday school facilities were adequate for holding twice as many students, but still its growth pattern followed the pattern taken by worship attendance.

Designate for worship a minimum of 25 percent of the money budgeted for member programs. Items included in this 25 percent are the bulletin, sheet music, cantatas, special musicians and instrumentalists, paraments, decor, and appearance. Do not include personnel such as choral director, sound engineers, or regularly paid musicians. Money spent on worship raises the satisfaction level of the congregation as much as anything a church can do.

Regularly emphasize attendance at worship. Instead of concentrating on church membership, encourage worship attendance. Usually, the larger the church becomes, the less percentage of membership attends services. Colonial Hills has accomplished just the opposite—the percent of members who attend worship is growing as we grow in membership. Since 1971 our worship attendance has grown 259 percent, and the ratio of worship attendance to membership has grown 2 percent, rather than declining. In 1988 our worship attendance averaged 47 percent of our membership, because we constantly reinforce the idea that worship is the most important ministry of the church.

Promote Sunday's sermon title and musical selections on the front page of the weekly newsletter. Announce special sermons, series, and musicals as far in advance as possible. Refer to Sunday as the first day of the week, rather than the last. List in the newsletter the names of those who attended church every Sunday the month before. Minimize events or schedules that would draw people away from attendance at worship. Throughout the year, invite different groups or ministries sponsored by the church to attend worship, both to be recognized and to have their ministry highlighted.

Worship is drama. Worship can be filled with good content, but unless that content is presented in a way that awakens the imagination and stirs the emotion of the congregation, seldom does anything lasting occur.

Like any good drama, worship must have movement that ebbs and flows, without long dead spots. The service must build to a final act and clamor for a response from the congregation. If the drama is well done, the congregation will become part of the cast of characters. The people will sense that everything is designed for their response. They will feel as if the final scene in the drama will be determined by what they do with their lives.

Those leading the worship are directors in the drama, more than participants. They must be aware of where the service is going and the intended outcome, and must not get lost in their individual parts.

Ushers and greeters are an effective part of the pastoral team. Ushers play a larger part in setting the stage for the worship drama than most of us realize. Where they seat people, when they allow people to enter, how they treat each person, how closely they monitor the room temperature and watch the needs of the congregation, the way they give out the bulletins, the closeness with which they work with the pastor—all these seemingly small concerns have a great deal to do with the comfort level of the people, and of the pastor.

Growth Principle Eight: Growth Usually Occurs with the Addition of Each New Morning Worship Service.

One of the best forms of stewardship is to begin a new service. An increase in worship attendance will usually occur within the first three months.

First United Methodist Church of Lafayette, Louisiana, is an old downtown church of 690 members. During the last ten years, First Church declined some 30 percent in membership and had been stable or declining in worship attendance. With the oil crash in 1986, the city's population declined from 130,000 to 110,000, and First Church lost 15 percent of its worship attendance. In September 1988, a second worship service was established at 8:00 A.M., and within three months, the worship attendance increased 20 percent.

Alamo United Methodist Church in the far eastern part of
Bexar County, Texas, has experienced this Growth Principle twice in the last eight years. In 1980 the congregation
began a second worship service, and attendance jumped
from 68 to 93 in six months, a 37 percent increase. In 1987, a
third worship service was offered, and attendance grew
from 144 to 168 in less than six months.

Consider a worship service at the same hour as Sunday school.
Because people are attending church earlier, a 9:00 or 9:30
worship service is growing in prominence and may take the
place of the traditional 10:30 or 11:00 service. The middle
service at Colonial Hills is our fastest growing service, and
at times is almost as large as the later service. It is a myth
that such a service will hurt attendance at Sunday school. If
anything, it will increase Sunday school attendance in the
children's department.

Don't forget Joe. He is going to drop off his children for
Sunday school and return an hour later to get them. If there
is a convenient service of worship at the same time as
Sunday school, he may be tempted to stay. If he does, don't
begrudge the fact that he is not going to Sunday school.
Take advantage of the fact that he is in worship. Give him a
grace period. Let the pastor preach to him, the congregation
love him, and maybe in time, Joe will be involved in Sunday
school. A high percentage of professions of faith and
restorations at Colonial Hills occur in this earlier service.

*Additional growth will occur in a service of worship if a choir is
provided.* Special music such as quartets, solos, or handbells
does not provide the same appeal as a choir that meets the
one-to-ten ratio. Add a choir to a service, and the
attendance will increase by more than the simple number of
choir members.

The logistics for providing two or three full-time choirs
are difficult, but it can be done. Consider having a youth
choir at the early service. Colonial Hills' youth choir has
been the choir for our 8:30 A.M. service since 1970. If you have
three services, allow all the adults to rehearse together in
order to sing the same anthems at each service. During

rehearsal, choir members can indicate which service they will attend the next Sunday. Although this procedure is harder on the director, it does not increase the amount of time spent in rehearsal, and it provides flexibility and choice for the choir members.

First United Methodist Church in Spring Hill, Florida, is a classic example of the growth that will occur by adding a third worship service and providing a choir at all three. Ninety percent of the worshiping congregation at Spring Hill is over fifty years of age. In the last ten years, the area has experienced more than 300 percent growth—mostly young adults—while the church had grown only 54 percent. In 1988, the church averaged 606 in worship, but one year later, the average was 694. According to pastor Lyman H. Kirkwood, the new 9:30 A.M. service proved so popular—225 average attendance—that in another year it may be the primary service. The 8:00 A.M. and 11:00 A.M. choirs practice together, then split up on Sunday. A folk choir sings at 9:30, giving a variety of worship experience. A youth choir sings at each service on a regular basis, and the associate pastor preaches one of the services on a rotating basis. It will be interesting to see if the new 9:30 A.M. service brings down the average age of the worshiping congregation.

In 1984 new emphasis was added to the early morning worship service at Wesley United Methodist Church in Harlingen, Texas, by providing special music and a separate bulletin. The result: Average attendance increased from 47 in 1984 to 138 in 1988.

Colonial Hills has added a choir to a new service of worship twice, and both times our worship attendance increased dramatically. Most recently, in 1986 a regular choir was added to our middle service, which was averaging 110. In two years it grew to an average of more than 260, a 137 percent increase! And the satisfaction level of the congregation rose equally.

Conclusion

Few things influence the growth of a church as much as the quality of worship. Of all the areas of church life, worship should receive the most attention. When worship meets the needs of people, the church will grow.

CHAPTER FIVE

God Wants the Church to Grow

I tell you, there will be more joy in heaven over one sinner who repents than over ninety-nine righteous persons who need no repentance.

—Luke 15:7

*T*HE ATTITUDES OF THE PASTOR, THE STAFF, AND THE CONGREGATION ARE THE MOST IMPORTANT FACTORS IN CHURCH GROWTH. In the twenty-five years following World War II, these attitudes did not have as much effect on the health of the church as they do now. It was the "in" thing to go to a mainline Protestant church; now it isn't. In today's complex secular world, long-term growth occurs in mainline Protestant churches only if there is a positive attitude toward growth on the part of the pastor, the staff, and the congregation.

Recently, the General Board of Discipleship of The United Methodist Church published a study, *Parable Churches* by Ralph and Nell Mohney, which analyzed the ten fastest growing churches in United Methodism between 1908–1985. The report highlighted many aspects of growing churches, but one dominant characteristic stood out clearly from the rest. Nine of the ten churches earnestly expected and determined strategies for their churches' growth.

One point of clarification is needed. Throughout this chapter I will refer often to the laity as the "unpaid" staff. I call the laity unpaid staff because the same dedication and quality of leadership is required of lay people as of the paid staff, the only difference being in the amount of time spent.

Growth Principles

Growth Principle Nine: Growth Is Directly Related to the Leadership Strength of the Pastor.

The single most important factor in determining the growth of a church is the pastor's attitude about its mission. If the pastor believes that the mission of the church is to win people to Jesus Christ, and if the pastor personally works for that mission, the church will grow.

The importance of this growth principle is illustrated in the turnaround of 116-year-old Rayne Memorial United Methodist Church in uptown New Orleans. For more than twenty years, worship attendance and membership declined yearly. A number of factors accounted for this decline: the attitude of New Orleans toward institutional religion (with only 800 members, Rayne Memorial is the largest UMC church in the central city); no off-street parking; restrictions placed on facilities in a Historic District; a $5 million endowment, which discouraged most attempts at stewardship; and a five-year average pastoral tenure.

Clyde Frazier has been the pastor of Rayne Memorial for the past ten years, during which time the worship attendance has grown 13 percent, from 189 to 226; Sunday school has almost doubled, from 76 to 142; and the number of giving units has increased 20 percent. And much of this took place during difficult economic times.

What caused this turnaround?—primarily, the presence and influence of a long-term, capable pastor. I spent two days evaluating Rayne Memorial and could find no other reason for this growth. Dr. Frazier's leadership has brought stability. The laity trusts his leadership, and as a result the church has a spirit that nurtures growth. As the church begins to intentionally reach out into the community, it will grow even more.

Two pastors are responsible for the transition of Ben Hill United Methodist Church* from a dying, all-white church to a growing, all-black congregation. In the late 1960s, Paul Wohlgemoth carefully guided the congregation through the "white flight" from the Ben Hill area of Atlanta, Georgia, by visiting black families and intentionally appointing them to leadership positions. His leadership not only stopped the decline but helped the church grow.

In 1974, Ben Hill received its first black pastor, Cornelius Henderson. Under his vision and leadership, the church grew from an average attendance of less than 100 to 1,876 in 1986. Between 1980 and 1985, Ben Hill was the second-fastest growing church in United Methodism.

Trinity United Methodist Church in Denver, Colorado,* is one of the hundreds of old inner-city mainline churches that have steadily declined since the end of the 1960s. Between 1956 and 1980, membership at the 100-year-old church declined from 3,846 to 1,043. Under the leadership of James E. Barnes, the decline ended and Trinity now has 2,000 members. Most members would agree that the Reverend Barnes brought three strengths to this congregation: enthusiastic leadership, dynamic preaching, and administrative skills.

Barnes' business acumen is the real key to Trinity's recovery. Under his leadership the congregation sold its air rights over the property. The purchaser agreed to tear down one old building, construct new underground facilities, restore some of the historic facilities, and also gave the church a $2 million endowment.

The longer the pastoral tenure, the more growth is likely to occur. Pastors need to "bloom where they are planted." It was not until my seventh year at Colonial Hills that significant ministry began. By *significant*, I mean ministry that takes a congregation beyond the everyday boundaries of church life, charts new courses, experiments with new forms of meeting people's needs, and keeps the congregation on the cutting edge of society's problems. Our entrance into the Metropolitan Congregational Alliance is an example of significant social and political ministry. This controversial ministry did not occur until my eleventh year as pastor, after more than two years of preparation.

One of the most often expressed fears I hear from United Methodist laity in every part of this country is this: "We're afraid to step out and take a risk for fear our present pastor won't be here very long, and we might not get as good a replacement." Significant ministry doesn't just happen. It usually happens only when trust and continuity of vision are made possible by long pastorates.

Long pastorates require two things. Longer and more flexible time away from the church is needed for vacation; for objective reflection on life in general and the church in particular; for development of fresh, relevant sermons; and for strategic planning. Pastors who have developed leaders among the laity can afford to be away from the church for extended periods of time. Most summers, though I may be gone seven to eight weeks at a time, the ministry goes on. I return with the basis for a year's worth of sermons and a strategy for action that is based on reflection, not on reaction.

Long pastorates also require pastors who experience regular personal growth so that the church does not outgrow them; they are always one step ahead, with fresh new ideas. I've seen pastors who did not grow in their skills, and the positions outgrew them so that they had to be replaced. They ministered well for several years, but they did not experience regular personal growth, and life passed them by.

The pastor's main role is to hold up a vision large enough to cause individuals to grow. Although the details of this vision vary from church to church, the driving force behind all such visions is a twofold belief system. First, our vision will determine our future. The future of the church is always in God's hands. It is never dependent upon what may happen. Pastors with vision believe that with God's help, they can change the future.

Second, what can be is more important than what is or what has been. Pastors with vision know that fear of the unknown and embarrassment of the past should never be part of the church's plans in the present. When pastors understand, believe, and are willing to follow the power of this twofold belief system, there is no limit to what God can do.

The pastor must be a leader, not an enabler. Much has been written about the difficulty of defining a leader. But we know a leader when we see one. A leader is a person who has enough of a following to cause things to happen. A leader, as opposed to an enabler, is more than a resource person who gives assistance when asked but never takes charge when the ball is dropped.

Pastors often say, "I don't think it's my place to lead the way for the congregation on important decisions. After all, it's their church, not mine. They'll be here long after I'm gone." Pastors must assume leadership in the life of the congregation they serve. They should not think of themselves as pilgrims passing through. A congregation grows with a strong pastor who is comfortable in a leadership role.

Over the past three decades, mainline Protestants have learned that the enabler style of leadership seldom produces healthy churches. The roles played by Moses and Aaron in the wilderness illustrate the difference between a leader and an enabler. Aaron *enabled* the people to do whatever they wanted to do, even to building a graven image. Moses *led* the people out of bondage into freedom.

The Moses model is helpful in describing pastoral leadership. Much of the basic idea for the following comments comes from *The Nursing Father: Moses as a Political Leader* by Aaron Wildavsky:

1. Pastors take people where they would not go on their own. Moses refused to allow the Hebrews to return to Egypt, but led them on to Canaan (see Exod. 32:1-10).

2. Pastors view life as one big learning experience. Moses learned from Pharaoh that it is deadly to make the same mistake twice (see Exod. 6:1-13).

3. Pastors make themselves unnecessary. Moses prepared others to carry on without him (see Deut. 34:1-9).

4. Pastors share authority; there is strength in numbers. Moses gathered seventy elders to help lead the people (see Num. 11:24-30).

5. The chief wisdom of pastoral leadership is to know that even when you feel you are right, you could be wrong. Moses prayed before he responded to Korah (see Num. 16:1-4).

The Pastor must be careful not to get too far out in front of the congregation. The pastor must understand and communicate with every part of the congregation. In addition to the normal one-on-one contact with the various unpaid staff of the church, I have found some methods helpful in providing communication to and from the pastor.

Twice each year, extend an open invitation to the congregation to participate in a Pastor's Dialogue on some issue that faces the church. Frame the meeting by informing the group why you've taken a certain position on an issue and let them respond. You will find that often the dialogue will begin with the laity sharing the kinds of goals and ministry they would like to see over the next few years. As another helpful method, take ten or fifteen minutes at each board or session meeting to share an idea and get a reaction. Often the spiritual health of the congregation can be measured by that reaction. It helps to visit, every third year, in the home of one hundred selected new members, long-time members, leaders, and potential leaders. The pastor also can stay in touch through casual conversation with selected members of the church.

The pastor should give the people what they need, rather than what they think they want. The pastor needs to know the difference. This style of leadership is obviously subjective and calls for regular evaluation on the part of the pastor. Without this distinction, the tendency of congregations would be never to venture into uncharted waters, and pastors would never subject themselves to some disciplines they might otherwise attempt.

An example of this kind of direction came in 1981 when I asked Colonial Hills to join the controversial Metropolitan Congregational Alliance. I could not find any member who wanted to join, including myself. But a few of us knew that an inclusive ministry must include social justice. We knew too that people like us needed to be involved in confronting the root causes of that injustice. And we also knew that joining would slow the growth of the church. The majority of the board did not want to join, but they did so unanimously because I asked them to, and they trusted me.

The pastor's style of leadership is determined by the size of the congregation (see Figure 4). Lack of understanding of the effect of congregational size on the leadership style required of the pastor is one of the main causes of church decline and stagnation. To take a small-church pastoral style into a middle- or large-sized church without first acquiring the necessary new leadership skills is, at best, frustrating; at worst, disastrous.

Small- to middle-sized churches (0-200 attendance at worship) require versatile entrepreneurial leadership. The pastor must be able to give leadership to several different programs and personalities. Since there is seldom any paid staff, the pastor must be willing to initiate programs and do those things no one else wants to do. The pastor must be a doer, a catalyst, a risk taker—an entrepreneur who works as a partner with the members on all kinds of projects.

Middle- to large-sized churches (200–500 at worship) require a pastor who can prioritize and act on what is important, ignoring the not-so-important. Because such sized churches usually do not provide adequate program staff, the pastor must be able to prioritize what the church will do and what it will neglect. This requires a pastor who can anticipate, adjust to, and interpret change to the congregation. The pastor functions mainly as a Chief Operating Officer.

Large to very large churches (500–900 at worship) require a pastor who is secure enough to delegate to a staff most matters except those that have long-range significance for the entire congregation. Large churches often stagnate because the pastors refuse to delegate authority to initiate and act. As a church grows, the variety of demands outgrows one person's ability to respond in a timely manner. Often pastors of large churches keep the program from growing beyond their ability to manage it personally, and it does not keep pace with the growing needs of the people. During this stage of development a pastor's main role is to hold up a vision larger than life; to make the hard decisions no one else wants to make; to do less actual "hands on" work and spend more time developing strategy. Such a pastor functions more as a Chief Executive Officer.

CAUTION: Delegation does not mean abdication of responsibility. In the method that works best at Colonial Hills, the paid staff and the congregation decide on the overall objectives of the church; then the members of the staff reach those objectives in their own way. The more creative and mature the staff, the more beneficial this method of delegation. In addition, the congregation must provide adequate salaries to attract the kind of staff that can assume this kind of responsibility.

Churches with more than 900 at worship may want the senior pastor to function more as Chairman of the Board. In this style, the pastor delegates everything except those issues that have a long-term effect on the church. The primary duties are preaching, teaching, and developing strategy, with very little hands on supervision, except when the pastor intentionally wishes to observe the way a staff person carries on day-to-day operations.

The pastor's style, no matter what size the church, must be versatile. Today Christians are experiencing and expressing their faith in a greater variety of ways than ever before. Such variety requires pastors who do not have a narrow, focused vision.

Figure 4: Church Size vs. Pastoral Style

CHURCH SIZE (Worship)	PASTORAL STYLE NEEDED
Small to Medium 0–200	Entrepreneur Versatile Partner
Medium to Large 200–500	Chief Operating Officer Prioritize and Act
Large to Very Large 500–900	Chief Executive Officer Delegater
Mega 900 +	Chairman of the Board Preacher and Strategist

Versatile pastors develop a balanced ministry that covers the spectrum of religious experience and expression, rather than making it necessary for churches to form around homogeneous groups of like-minded people. Versatile pastors are flexible enough to relate to the various parts of the church, even those not the pastor's main interest. Pastors must be secure enough in their faith to be able to trade dialogue with people of different persuasions. They must have standards, but never feel they have sole possession of the truth.

Versatile pastors become the glue that holds together the diverse parts of a growing church. Although this is true in all size churches, it is more true in larger churches. The pastor is one of the few, if not the only person in touch with a broad spectrum of the congregation, the visitors, and perhaps the community. The pastor mediates and interprets between the various parts of the church to make sure all interests are heard equally and shared.

Versatile pastors build up a network of relationships throughout the congregation and become effective power brokers. They should not avoid using this power. The pastor who acts as if the use of power has never entered his or her mind is more dangerous to the health of the congregation than the pastor who is aware of that power and seeks to use it wisely. Rather than avoiding the exercise of power, pastors need to learn the difference between personal power and social power. Personal power is the desire to serve one's own profit or ego. Social power is used to bring about good for everyone. Pastors need to remember that good things don't just happen—they are caused to happen. That's social power. Don't be afraid to be a power broker for the good of the church.

Pastors should know when it is time to move on. As a rule, pastors should seldom think of moving. However, both pastor and congregation need an agreed-upon way to determine when it is time to move. I suggest the following: Divide your ministry into three stages.

Stage One includes the beginning of your ministry in a local church. As long as there is steady growth, don't even think of moving. Stage Two consists of growth, stagnation, and decline. During this period, you and the congregation should constantly evaluate, develop strategy, and determine what causes the ups and downs. As long as the growth pattern is up and down, don't move. Level periods are often times for the birth of new and exciting ministries. In Stage Three, a pattern of steady decline begins. When such a decline reaches 10 percent of the total attendance at worship, it is time to move.

There are exceptions to this cycle: if the pastor's health is endangered by the pressure of growth; if the goals of the pastor and the congregation grow apart; if there are large shifts in the population.

Growth Principle Ten: Growth Is Directly Related to the Attitude of the Paid Staff.

Growing churches staff for growth rather than for decline or maintenance. Churches find that use of paid staff not only pays for itself, but also pays for facilities, programs, and missions.

An analysis of Colonial Hills shows the major importance of pastor and/or staff in sustained growth. In 1969 a change in pastors at Colonial Hills stopped a two-year decline in worship attendance, and a rapid recovery resulted in a new sanctuary within eighteen months. From 1975 through 1978, the church did not add any staff and, as a result, experienced five years of minimal growth. But in 1979, Colonial Hills made a commitment to a large multiple staff and began a substantial period of sustained growth. By 1986, most members of the staff had had at least three years to develop their ministry; the result was that the church grew more in 1986 than in the previous four years combined (see Chart 3 in Appendix).

Every time staff was added, growth occurred in the program area. It didn't grow between 1975 and 1977 because we didn't staff for growth (see Chart 4 in Appendix).

The crucial importance of pastor and staff is true for all size churches. Small- to middle-sized congregations seldom have a person or a group with enough objectivity to see beyond what is, to what can be. Small congregations tend to be ingrown and survival oriented. Only someone from the outside can see the possibilities. The pastor of a small church who wants to see the congregation grow will need to risk and exercise strong leadership, or the church will remain small and vulnerable.

Middle- to large-sized congregations are most likely to be confused about the relationship of pastor and staff to church growth. As a rule, people do not change their attitudes quickly. So as the church grows, staff and members do not always adjust their understanding of the roles that growth demands of them. The tendency of members is to remember either the way things were or the kind of church they came from. This size church needs a staff that can adjust to change and interpret it to the congregation.

Figure 5: Relationship Between Stages of a Growing Church and Skills Needed

*STAGE OF DEVELOP-MENT	TENDENCY IN ATTITUDE	LEADERSHIP OF CHURCH PROCESS	REASON DEVELOPMENT	NECESSARY PASTORAL SKILLS
Small to Medium 0–200	Survival "Water Testers" "We can't do that."	Recruiting	Ministry larger than pool	Catalyst Change Agent Risk taker Partnership Entrepreneurial
Medium to Large 200–500	Resistance to change: "We have arrived."	Training	Difficulty assimilating change. Pastoral staff overworked, ministry understaffed	Anticipates, adjusts to & interprets change. Chief Operating Officer. Prioritize
Large to Very Large 500–900	Confused about role of staff, laity, policy, procedure	Identifying	Large size & unknown quantity of pool	Visionary Decision-maker. CEO/Chairman of The Board. Delegation
Mega 900 +	Aloof Cold Fragile Traditional	Deploying	Reliance on staff; not enough staff	Chairman of the Board. Preacher and Strategist

*Denotes Average Worship Attendance

Large and mega congregations depend heavily upon the skills and vision of the staff. Members tend not to understand that additional staff makes it possible for more laity to be in mission. The larger the church, the more impossible it is for one person or one group to have enough relationships to command the kind of trust necessary to

motivate significant ministry. A large church must have a
staff that is willing to take major leadership responsibility
for networking the congregation. Figure 5 summarizes the
relationship between the growing stages of a church and
the pastoral/staff skills needed.

*The primary role of the program staff is to identify, recruit,
train, deploy, and lead the laity in mission.* The larger the staff,
the more lay people will be in mission. Program staff
members never take the place of laity, but use every
program as an opportunity to involve new people in
mission and identify future unpaid staff. The end product
of every program is the spiritual development of people,
not the accomplishment of a task.

*People-centered ministry requires one paid program staff person
for every 100 persons in worship, or every 300 members on the roll,
whichever is greater.* Growing churches that want to remain
warm and caring will do well to follow this formula; only
100 to 150 people can be effectively networked by one
person each year. Understaffing is one reason large
churches appear unfriendly and lose a higher percentage of
members to inactivity. At Colonial Hills, 47 percent of the
members attend worship; it has a low drop-out rate and a
warm and caring attitude because there is one paid program
staff member for every 100 people in worship (see Chart 5 in
Appendix).

Paid program staff includes anyone who is directly
involved in planning and implementing program, not
counting business managers or weekday kindergarten or
day-care directors. This ratio assumes that each paid staff
person is full-time; two part-time people are considered as
one full-time. The more complex the ministry of a church, the
more important it is that this ratio is the minimum standard.

Even though the type of position and the order in which
the position is added is determined by the particular
ministry needs of each local congregation, some broad
guidelines apply. For a congregation that has between 100
and 200 in worship, the first staff person to be added is a
full-time secretary. This size church often makes the

mistake of adding a part-time youth director first. This makes the pastor a very expensive secretary and also gives a bad image to the community when people call during working hours and no one answers the phone. At 200 in worship, an associate pastor is necessary for adequate pastoral coverage and time for personal pastoral development.

Churches between 300 and 400 in worship need a full-time director of music capable of developing and shepherding a large quality choir and music ministry. Churches with more than 500 in worship also need a business administrator who can relieve the pastor of administrative duties as well as give solid financial direction. (Smaller churches that fill this position show more concern for the institution than for people.) With more than 700 in worship, churches need extra pastoral care to assure stability, keep in touch with the congregation, and keep the drop-out rate from increasing. The larger the church, the more important are the roles of associate pastor(s), senior pastor's secretary, and business administrator.

The choosing of paid staff should be the responsibility of the pastor. According to John Ed Mathison, pastor of Frazer Memorial United Methodist Church, "Picking the right people is my most important responsibility." He is referring to staff, volunteers, and even the nominating committee. He prefers to choose staff members from the thousands of volunteers at Frazer. By observing a person's commitment and ability as a volunteer, John Ed can tell whether that person will make a good staff member. A long pastorate makes it possible for this pastor to know the members well enough to make the right choices.

People-centered ministries require less support staff. Paid support staff consists of anyone not directly involved with planning and implementing programs. In a church where the emphasis is on people rather than on record keeping, the need for support staff is not as great as in an institutionally oriented church. A good rule of thumb is to have one paid support person for every program person.

The ratio of secretaries to program staff is best kept to one secretary for every two or three program staff members. The ratio of paid support staff to paid program staff is usually higher in small and large congregations than in middle-sized congregations. Many middle-sized congregations tend to be top-heavy with support staff, and as a result, their record keeping is better than their ministry to people.

Program staff people are the senior pastor's main source of information about the congregation. Because of their close working relationships with the laity, program staff members know segments of the congregation better than the pastor does. Consider these relationships during the yearly nominations; consult the staff members on a regular basis about what they are hearing in their various areas of responsibilities; include the staff in setting objectives and making major decisions, with the final decision being reserved for the senior pastor. At each staff meeting, ask, "What are you hearing that I need to know?"

The relationship of pastor to paid staff is that of quarterback and team. In 1984, the members of my staff came to a meeting wearing bright red T-shirts with A TEAM written across the front. I was presented with my own red T-shirt with QUARTERBACK on the front. A joke—yes—but more than just a joke. My T-shirt was a symbol of the relationship between pastor and staff. I was seen as the quarterback, not the coach.

There are two kinds of quarterbacks. One is sent the plays by the coach; the other calls the plays on the field. The pastor calls the plays on the field. The pastor is part of the team, but is also the one who runs the plays. While a play is being developed, staff members should be given the opportunity to participate by either questioning its validity or arguing for a different strategy. Staff meetings should be occasions for open dialogue between pastor and staff. But once the play has been called by the pastor, the staff should never gripe about the call in front of the other members.

In giving leadership to his staff, John Ed Mathison places

a high premium on team building, group support, and role modeling. On Wednesday the entire staff, including both program and support staff, meets for thirty to forty-five minutes. According to Mathison, "The complete team needs to know the objectives. The quarterback is no more important than the guard." This meeting is followed by a thirty- to forty-five-minute meeting of the lead program staff. In addition to these meetings, staff members meet for coffee every day and eat lunch together away from the church once a month.

There are two dimensions to the relationships among paid staff—relational and functional. Relational has to do with the personal relationships developed among the staff members. Functional has to do with accomplishing the mission. The more demanding the ministry, the more need to emphasize the relational needs of the staff.

The paid staff members at Colonial Hills lunch together each week prior to the regular staff meeting, giving us a chance to catch up on one another's lives. Once a year we go on retreat for two full days and spend the majority of that time together in recreation. The functional needs are met during the weekly staff meetings and the ten one-day work periods each year. The meeting agendas are set by the individual members of the staff in advance of the meetings. This allows the staff to have input and also allows the pastor to know where the staff is, in relation to the overall objectives of the congregation. On Sunday morning before the first service, we go over the order of worship and any special events of the day to assure that all special needs of the staff are addressed during worship.

Several criteria should be considered in selecting multiple staff. Whenever possible, choose talented lay people over clergy. Clergy are trained to be theologians and seldom have the needed skills in education, youth work, or business. The program staff at Colonial Hills has consistently contained a high percentage of talented laywomen.

Choose individuals who require the least supervision. The best staff member is a creative self-starter who can finish projects. If after three months on the job, a staff member still does not understand the job and requires an unusual amount of supervision, the loving response is to give that person a month's notice. Common sense and the ability to make decisions can't be taught. Often pastors who want to do the "Christian thing" wait too long before giving a person notice. The result is always the same—even though members of the staff know the person isn't working out, everyone feels guilty because a member of the "family" is being dismissed.

Higher salaries and a smaller staff are better than lower salaries and a larger staff. Do not try to hire program staff at the lowest possible salary. And avoid prima donnas, no matter how talented. They will cause dissension within the team and will not be representatives of the pastor within the congregation.

Part-time staff can give flexibility to the hiring process by allowing a congregation to fill positions as needs arise, then allow the positions and salaries to grow to full-time; hire from the growing pool of women who want to work and still be home with their children after school; participate in the growing interest in job time-sharing; concentrate the job description on a small enough area to hold the person accountable; and hire specialists rather than generalists. Keep in mind that dedicated and competent part-time people usually accomplish more than they are hired to do.

There are two major drawbacks to hiring part-time people: They require as much if not more supervision than full-time people, and they are harder to hold responsible, because the job often is too big for a part-time person.

Negotiate staff positions for as long a period as possible. We like to add new staff people on a three-year basis and give them three months to get a good grasp of the responsibilties. If at that point a person is not proving to be a creative self-starter and finisher, a month's notice is given. The same is true when a staff person begins to be nonproductive—one month's notice is given. If this procedure is followed, a three-year contract can produce the kind of quality programming a growing church must have in order to sustain growth. It will also allow staff people to be aware of their status with the senior pastor at all times.

Lead the staff by objective. "Responsible for the overall music ministry, including adult, youth, children, and bell choirs." With such a job description, there is no way to evaluate whether a person effectively carries out this directive. In leadership by objective, that same job description would read as follows: "Each adult and youth choir will average one person in the choir for every ten people in the worshiping congregation. Each children's choir will sing ten times during the calendar year. Bell choirs will perform no more than eight times during a calendar year. Highest priority goes to the quality and size of the eleven o'clock adult choir." With such job descriptions, staff people know what is expected and how to evaluate their own ministry. Leadership by objective requires a pastor who has both personal and congregational objectives that are clear and measurable. We will discuss ways to set objectives in the next chapter.

The larger the church, the more intentional communication must become between members of the paid staff. Set aside regular times when the program staff, the business adminstrator, and the senior pastor's secretary meet with the senior pastor to share objectives and personal needs. The senior pastor needs a regular forum in which to share overall objectives for the church, so that the objectives of each staff member are able to support and complement those objectives. The paid staff should have a regular forum to share objectives and ideas, so that the senior pastor and each member of the staff know the concerns, victories, defeats, and career needs of the other members.

Staff at all levels should have regular access to the pastor. It helps if a limited time each week is set aside just for appointments with the pastor. The larger the church, the more rigid the pastor may need to be in insisting that all staff people make appointments instead of just dropping in.

Communication should never become more important than the mission of the church.

The larger the staff, the more intentional the program staff must be in time management. Don't do anything your secretary can do for you! Let your secretary make appointments, find phone numbers, screen calls, open and answer mail, and file sermon material. Concentrate on the bread-and-butter priorities. Set your own agenda. Make short- and long-term objectives, and do not let the unexpected distract you from concentrating on and reaching those objectives. Return calls at your convenience. Set aside blocks of time for study. Don't stop what you're doing every time a member drops in to see you without an appointment. Unless in a rural area, use the phone whenever possible, instead of making a personal visit.

Schedule time away at your own pace. Use a Dictaphone instead of writing or dictating letters to a secretary. Communicate with other staff members through short, simple notes, instead of taking time to talk with them. Do what you do best instead of trying to improve your shortcomings. Pay a wedding coordinator to handle arrangements, including the rehearsal. Conduct group premarital counseling sessions. Provide general counseling on a short-term basis, with more serious situations contracted out to a qualified group of trained counselors.

Growth Principle Eleven: Growth Is Directly Related to the Unpaid Staff's Perception of the Congregation's Size and Ability, Rather Than the Reality.

Communicating to the congregation a *realistic* perception of a church's size is the single most important ministry the unpaid staff (lay leadership) can perform. What the unpaid staff *perceives* as reality usually determines the scope of the church's ministry. Most often the unpaid staff think of their church as much smaller and weaker than it really is, and as a result, such a church offers weak and ineffective ministries.

Once a congregation has adopted a common vision, it is the role of the unpaid staff to realize that vision in ways that meet the needs of the congregation. The unpaid staff must be able to suspend judgment long enough to assimilate new data, formulate new priorities, and act for the common good rather than personal preference. Even though members may disagree with their leaders, they will respect and follow them because they know those leaders have listened to all sides of the issue before offering an opinion. People have an opinion or bias about almost everything, but when the leaders of the church come together, it is essential that opinions be set aside so that objective decisions can be made.

University United Methodist Church in urban Syracuse, New York,* reached a high in worship attendance of 320 in 1959, then declined to a low of 160 in 1979. That year, a handful of lay people decided that Univeristy could grow again. They promoted a "can do" attitude which they called bubble-up theology. In bubble-up theology, the laity is turned loose to do its thing. The role of the pastor is to fan the fire.

As a result, a twenty-year decline was ended. Worship attendance is now 200 and rising, and Sunday school attendance averages 110, from a low of 60 in 1978. These figures are impressive when compared to the general trend in this area of the country.

Following this bubble-up theology, University is known for its outreach ministry: helping needy people in the area link up with an agency designed to meet their needs. It also participates in refugee resettlement, Habitat for Humanity, and the Sandwich Brigade. The spirit of bubble up has brought a renewal of the inner journey with meditation, Bible study, and spiritual-growth groups.

Unpaid staff members are the ministers of the church. Train and encourage the laity to do as much actual caring for one another as possible.

First United Methodist Church in Plymouth, Michigan,* is located in an area where most denominations are reporting membership decline. In 1984, this 1,375-member congregation began to gain about 60 net members a year. The congregation attributes this to two things: the arrival of a new pastor and the church's emphasis on members actually caring for one another. All forms of lay ministry are encouraged. As a result, mission giving is up from $1,000 to $34,000 beyond apportionments, and the congregation is planning a $3 million program to enlarge the facilities. There is even talk of expansion plans in the year 2000.

A former Evangelical United Brethren church encourages its unpaid staff members to do the work of ministry by sharing their story of faith wherever they go. Lake Magdalene United Methodist Church,* located in the Tampa area, grew from 430 attendance at worship in 1980 to 1,100 in 1988. In an effort to share its story with the community, the church surveyed the needs of the area and developed programs on death and dying, divorce and separation, parents and teens, single-parent homes, and parenting skills. Each of these programs becomes a vehicle through which the members can tell what their faith means to them.

Unpaid staff must be able to accept and appreciate people with different viewpoints (instead of just tolerating them). A healthy congregation will have a wide range of views and life-styles. There is a correlation between familiarity with the institutional church and an inability to accept people with differing viewpoints. The longer a person has been active in the institutional church, the more likely that person is to be critical of people with different opinions. Liberals can be just as intolerant as fundamentalists. So when choosing leadership, lean toward people in the middle of the road, not institutionally oriented.

A growing church in a complex, fast-paced world demands an unpaid staff with a high level of energy. Unpaid staff people must be accessible to the congregation—take time to listen to a wide range of viewpoints, be friendly with large segments of the congregation, and act on issues in such a way that others will know that these people will listen. In a church with more than one worship service, leaders should rotate the services they attend.

Limit the tenure of the unpaid staff. Rotate leadership every two or three years. Limited tenure makes it easier for people to make a commitment; allows new leaders to surface with new ideas; insures that the paid staff does not settle in and stagnate; helps prevent power cliques; and insures that a higher percentage of leaders are new to your church.

A balanced, growing church requires one unpaid leader for every fifteen members of the congregation. There are five steps in the process of developing more unpaid staff—identifying, recruiting, training, deploying, and leading. Each step is separate and must be intentionalized. The size of the congregation will determine which step is most crucial for each church.

In small to medium churches (0–200 worship attendance), the most important step is recruitment, because the pool of volunteers is always larger than the program. In middle to large churches (200–500 worship attendance), training is most important, because the paid staff is usually overworked, the program understaffed, and the church expects better quality than before. In large to very large churches (500–900 worship attendance), identifying potential leaders is the most difficult part of the process because of the many new or unknown members. Large churches tend to have such a large pool of talent to draw from that undeveloped talent is often overlooked. Mega churches (900+ in worship) find deployment the greatest obstacle, since unpaid staff tend to rely on paid staff to do the work of the church. This attitude is encouraged because of a lack of paid staff to develop the appropriate networks.

It is best if paid staff is in charge of either all or part of this process. Unpaid staff people simply do not have the time or the networks to do an adequate job of identifying, recruiting, training, and deploying volunteers. Unpaid staff members should work closely with the paid staff and also should receive far more consideration than the members who have not yet invested enough of their time to be knowledgeable about their church.

Conclusion

A growing, balanced church requires a congregational commitment to a strong paid and unpaid staff. It requires a pastor and paid staff people who, over a long period of time, hold up a vision that takes the congregation into ministries it might not choose on its own. It requires a small but dedicated support staff, and a mature unpaid staff that can take the larger-than-life vision and make it happen in ways that benefit the entire congregation.

CHAPTER SIX

God Expects Our Best

Jesus said, "He who believes in me . . . greater works than these will he do."

—John 14:12

GROWING CHURCHES ARE COMMITTED TO MEETING THE NEEDS OF BOTH CHURCHED AND UNCHURCHED PEOPLE. Whatever your church expects from the members, it will receive. If members are approached with the attitude that what they are asked to do isn't very important, qualified people will refuse; the unqualified will accept but do very little. When you have high expectations of every person in the church, you bring out their best by challenging them to do more than they think they can accomplish.

In 1976, Colonial Hills was disturbed by the casual attitude of our Sunday school teachers toward their classroom responsibilities. They would show up on Sunday morning if it were convenient; routinely call to cancel as late as Saturday; not be in their classes early to prepare for the students. As a result, teachers were difficult to recruit and to keep, Sunday school was a low priority for the students, and parents complained that their children and youths did not want to attend Sunday school.

We addressed this problem by developing The Committed Best concept. Sunday school is treated with the same importance as public school. Teachers are expected to be adequately trained, faithful in attendance, and in class

78

fifteen minutes early. They also are expected to attend special classes and workshops to keep their skills sharp.

We developed a training course called Basic Christian Tools. The course was designed to meet once a week for nine months. The curriculum, developed by the pastors, covered all the information resources needed to teach in a Christian school. The first year, 75 people enrolled. At the end of the second year, we didn't have enough classrooms for the people who wanted to teach! Saturday-night cancellations dropped to a minimum; teachers were in their classrooms early; children began to learn; and complaints declined drastically.

Today, prior to entering the classroom, teachers and a representative from the congregation sign a covenant stating that both parties agree to live up to certain expectations (see Chart 6 in Appendix). During a service of consecration, the teachers place their covenants on the altar. The pastors lay hands on each teacher, saying, "Take thou authority to teach the Word of God." Here a clear statement is made—Sunday school teachers are expected to do their best in the classroom.

Over the years, The Committed Best concept has been expanded to include every area of leadership. Everyone who holds a leadership position is asked to sign a Committed Best covenant, and all new leaders attend our annual two-day leadership conference. It is clear to both paid and unpaid staff that their church expects their committed best (see Charts 7, 8, 9 in Appendix).

Growth Principles

Growth Principle Twelve: When 80 Percent of Any Space Is in Use, It Is Time to Start Making Plans for More.

Growing churches reach a critical window of opportunity when they reach 80 percent capacity in any area. Colonial Hills uses 80 percent as a "triggering" device. As soon as we reach that capacity, we begin plans for additional facilities.

We've found that the sooner a growing congregation responds to the 80-percent rule and provides more space, the easier it will be for the congregation to pay for the addition; the longer a congregation waits to respond, the harder it will be. When a church exceeds the 80-percent rule, it is beyond the comfort zone that is acceptable to most people; every other Sunday, it is uncomfortably full; on special Sundays, intolerably crowded. It sends a signal to the community that it is out of room.

Between 1977 and 1982, St. James United Methodist Church in Little Rock, Arkansas, averaged 13 percent growth a year in worship attendance. By 1982 the church had exceeded its 80 percent capacity. A new sanctuary was completed in 1982, with 100 new parking spaces, and worship attendance increased some 34 percent the first year.

Alamo United Methodist Church, as mentioned before, has experienced the result of this growth principle twice. In 1980, the congregation reached 80 percent capacity and began a second worship service, jumping from 68 to 93 in attendance. In 1987, 80 percent capacity was again reached; when a third worship service was offered, attendance grew from 144 to 168.

The five main areas of concern to the 80-percent rule are the amount of land owned by the church; parking; and the capacity of the sanctuary, the nursery, and the Sunday school. Keep careful statistics on each, review them at least quarterly, and follow the 80-percent rule. This will ensure that growth does not take money away from the essential ministries—Christian nurture, evangelism, social action, and missions.

If you don't know the exact capacity of your sanctuary, don't rely on an architect's estimate. Ask a group of people to fill one pew to capacity. Measure that pew and the remaining pews, and determine the capacity based on the pew you filled with people. Do not include folding chairs, foyer, overflow areas, aisles, any space that does not have an adequate view of the chancel area or that clearly is not part of the sanctuary proper. If your seating consists entirely of folding chairs, the total number of chairs would be the capacity, and 80 percent of that total would be considered comfortably full.

It is common to see membership figures growing while worship attendance remains stagnant. During the last five years, Asbury United Methodist Church in Corpus Christi, Texas, has grown in membership from 443 to 706, while attendance at worship has remained at 321. Sunday school attendance peaked at 203 in 1987. Both plateaus are due to the 80-percent rule.

Many of our larger and older churches are good examples of the way the rule affects growth. First United Methodist Church of Hurst, Texas, had an 80 percent sanctuary capacity of 300. For ten years, attendance at the main worship hour remained a constant 380, while membership grew from 2,342 to 3,084. Hurst will be worth watching, due to the construction of a larger sanctuary (which was needed fifteen years ago). After completion of the new sanctuary in 1988, attendance at the main worship service increased from 380 to 503 in three months.

Know the capacity for each Sunday school classroom. Allocate thirty square feet for each child in first grade and younger, and twenty square feet for everyone else, including adults. Divide this number into the square feet of each room, then multiply by .80 to get the 80 percent figure. In considering the needs of adults, take into consideration such things as table arrangement, desired fellowship, and design of each class.

Make sure worship capacity is 50 percent larger than educational space. Adding Sunday school space does not promote numerical growth, nor will it pay for itself. Churches grow and pay for their growth through worship services. Too often, churches make the mistake of providing more educational space than their worship space can afford.

Calculate the ratio of worship to educational space according to the way a church functions. The ratio is easy to determine for churches that have only one worship service and one Sunday school hour. However, churches with multiple services that overlap Sunday school find the calculation more complicated because of the need to consider better flow patterns for both people and cars, as well as additional parking needs. While it is less expensive to add more services than to build larger facilities, it requires more money for traffic flow and parking.

Next to the sanctuary, the nursery is the most important area of the church. A full nursery is not good for a growing congregation, especially at a time when so many first-time mothers are bringing their children to church. Few mothers feel comfortable leaving their children in the nursery for the first time, no matter how nice it might be, much less when it is overcrowded.

Prepare a brochure that tells parents how often the toys are cleaned and linens changed. The attendants should wear clean, neat uniforms. Teenagers should never be the leader or the primary source of staffing. Take pictures of first-time babies and send them to the parents on their first anniversary in the church. Have a staff person visit all newborns and leave a gift from the church, such as a book on caring for infants.

Growth Principle Thirteen: Growth Is Encouraged When Parking Is Adequate.

Parking is the most overlooked physical deterrent to church growth, as well as the hardest growth principle to impress upon congregations. Approximately 90 percent of mainline Protestant churches have a serious parking problem.

First United Methodist Church in Brownsville, Texas, opened a brand new facility in 1974, with 1,000 members. Good planning had gone into the initial site acquisition, but when the new facility opened, a very small hard-surface parking lot was provided—one that was barely half the size necessary to support the seating capacity of the sanctuary.

By 1982, the membership had declined to 500. The decision was made to spend $50,000 to double the parking capacity.

"We have no alternative, unless we are interested in dwindling further and finally dying,"voiced the chairperson of the planning committee. With the added parking, the church began to grow steadily, until by 1986 it had 997 members, with an average worship attendance of 482.

Suburban churches need a minimum of eight acres of land. The vast majority of the few growing churches in mainline Protestantism are finding that a major hindrance to growth is a shortage of land for off-street parking. When churches were established in 1960, four acres of land was considered adequate. Several factors have changed over the last twenty-five years, making it necessary for churches to have a minimum of eight acres. For example, most relationships are formed outside the neighborhood, such as at work or the health club; America's love affair with the automobile makes it easy for people to drive ten to twenty miles to a church that suits their particular needs; many families attend church in more than one car; more and more Americans are looking for large churches that can offer specialized ministries.

In 1983, the congregation of First United Methodist Church of Round Rock, Texas, was worshiping in a small facility with no off-street parking. People had to park as far away as four blocks. In 1984, the congregation moved to a school where there was plenty of parking and worship increased from 300 to 409. Two years later, the congregation moved to its permanent campus of seven acres. Very quickly, phase one of parking was full; phase two was completed within one year and it too was full; and now phase three of parking has been completed. The church has gone to three worship services to spread out the parking needs. In 1989, the church averaged 587 in worship and was considering a fourth phase of parking to keep up with the congregation's growth.

In 1973, Colonial Hills had a chance to purchase seven

adjacent acres at $10,000 an acre. We refused it then, again
in 1977 at $30,000 an acre, and again in 1980 at $100,000 an
acre. In 1985 we bought the last four acres of adjacent land at
$250,000 an acre! We immediately paved one acre to provide
parking for 150 cars. Within six months the spaces were full.
We added an additional 50 spaces, which were full within
one year. As a result, our 1986 worship attendance grew 13
percent, compared with 9 percent in 1985. Our growth in
worship attendance for the twelve months after providing
additional parking space was greater than it had been in
1982–1983 just after building a new sanctuary (see Chart 10
in Appendix).

Max seldom understands the importance of providing
adequate parking because he is accustomed to the days
when on-street parking was acceptable and people walked
several blocks to church; usually comes to church early and
stays late, so there is always adequate parking; has not
assimilated the relationship of the cultural changes in
America to church attendance.

Downtown churches need parking too! First United Methodist Church of Wichita, Kansas, is a textbook example of a
downtown church that has developed adequate parking.
During the 1970s, First Church, under the guidance of now
Bishop Richard Wilke, gave priority to the steady acquisition of all available real estate around its buildings. Because
of these expensive provisions for parking, the church had
record growth during the 1980s. It will be interesting to see
if it continues its commitment as it inches closer to
inadequate parking.

There are seven steps in determining how many parking
spaces your church needs. Each year, take a written survey
during worship service for four consecutive weeks (but not
on a holiday weekend). "How many people came to church
this morning in your car?" Make sure each driver fills out
the survey every Sunday, even if he or she has filled out the
form the previous Sunday. Divide the average person-per-
car into the largest hour of attendance to find the number of
parking spaces needed. For example, if worship and

Sunday school occur at the same time, that probably will be the hour of highest attendance. Then count the number of off-street paved parking spaces. Compute the 80-percent factor to determine the number of spaces available. Compare the total parking spaces needed with the total parking spaces available. And remember the 80-percent rule!

Growth Principle Fourteen: Growth Can Occur Even Though a Church Cannot Afford to Build.

Colonial Hills has expanded its facilities once every twelve months during the last twenty years, and not once were we able to make the mortgage payment upon completion of the project. But because we believed in the future, we raised enough money to pay the debt service for one year, and after building, we always grew enough to add the debt service to the budget by the end of the year. If we had waited to expand until we had the money, we would have missed the windows of opportunity, and the projects would have caused tremendous financial difficulties, just as when we waited too long to purchase the land. In waiting so long, we missed several windows of opportunity, and as a result, our growth plateaued out between 1975 and 1978, the cost of the land went up over 2,000 percent, and our outreach ministries suffered for two years.

The following procedure works extremely well. First, estimate the yearly amortization of the amount of expansion your church considers necessary to exceed the 80-percent requirement. Next, evaluate the different methods of financing a long-term loan, and then arrange for total financing of the entire project. We have always used bonds rather than borrowing from banks or savings and loans. If the members purchase bonds, they are more likely to show an interest in the health of the church. Finally, begin raising enough cash to take care of six to eighteen months of yearly mortgage payments. When you have this amount, start construction.

All the cash on hand a growing church needs to begin construction is an amount necessary to make six to eighteen mortgage payments, depending on the size of the church and its potential for growth. If the debt approaches three times the annual budget, it is better to plan on eighteen months. This procedure allowed Colonial Hills to grow and take advantage of the windows of opportunity before we needed to include extra debt in the budget.

Growth Principle Fifteen: Growth Can Occur Without
Merely Transferring Members from One
Church to Another.

Adult professions of faith are the focus of biblical church growth. We do an injustice to our biblical heritage when our primary source of church growth is infant baptism, or the confirmation of children, or the transfer of people from one church to another. As important as these actions are, they are not the main source for biblical growth.

In most denominations, adults are added to the church rolls in one of three ways: profession of faith and restoration (rededication); transfer by letter from the same denomination; or transfer from another denomination. The goal at Colonial Hills has been to reach the point where the number of people who join by profession of faith and restoration equals those who join by transfer of any kind. In 1987, 124 of 250 new members joined by profession of faith and restoration.

Examples of mainline Protestant churches that have a large number of people who join by profession of faith are hard to find. But when one is found, it is always growing.

One-third of Frazer Memorial's new members have joined by profession of faith. When Jack Thompson began to direct the church-growth program in 1974, most additions were by transfer from other churches, and most professions of faith were by confirmation. There were only 23 adult professions of faith. But in 1988, 223 joined by profession of faith. Remembering how excited he was about his own conversion, Jack had changed their outreach tactics. Goals were set, and members involved in evangelism were asked to make the unchurched their top priority. Intentional effort was made to find adults who would give their lives to Christ during the worship service. The leadership did not assume that visitors were faithful disciples. People who had gotten away from religion were encouraged to respond to their need to get back into the faith. As people slowly began to respond, an openness to adult conversions began to develop throughout the congregation. Now adult professions of faith are a regular occurrence at Frazer Memorial.

Dan Bonner was the pastor of First United Methodist Church in Brownsville, Texas, and is now pastor of First United Methodist Church in Wichita, Kansas. In both churches, well over one-half of all new members enter by profession of faith or reinstatement. When asked why, Dr. Bonner said,

> These churches train the lay people to invite friends to visit their Sunday school classes, home study and support groups, and social activities within the church programs. Most active church members are personal friends or close acquaintances of people who have no active Christian faith. The central strategy of encouraging members to invite friends, acquaintances, and family members opens the door for these undisciplined people to experience in the warmth of a Christian group what it means to accept Christ. Evangelical worship, with an invitation to personal commitment in each service, is an essential ingredient in the formula. But people commit their lives to Christ because they were first invited by a friend or close acquaintance to experience what it means to be a Christian.

Congregations can determine their potential for biblical church growth in several ways. First, check the census figures for the schools in your area of the city or county. If the census figures have increased, there is no reason your church shouldn't grow. (The form of ministry or social makeup of the people reached may need to change.) Next, by surveying the worshiping congregation over four consecutive weeks, define the area that is presently being served by your church. Ask how many miles the members drive to work and to church, as well as the time it takes to do both. People will drive to church almost the same number of miles or length of time it takes to get to work. If they are driving an average of ten miles to work and only three miles to church, there is need to concentrate on that seven-mile radius.

Using the data from that survey, draw an imaginary circle around your church, equal to the number of miles your members drive to work. Sixty percent of the people in that circle are not in church on any given Sunday and are potential members of your church.

Next, determine what kind of people live within that area. The categories to consider are singles never married, single-parent families, singles divorced, young families, older families, senior citizens, youth, upper/middle/lower class, black/white/brown/yellow/red. You can get most of this information from your Chamber of Commerce, city planning office or from private demographic firms. Finally, determine which of those groups are not being ministered to adequately by any church from your denomination, and develop ministries to meet their needs.

Colonial Hills began its singles ministry this way. Our studies in 1980 revealed that a high percentage of nearby apartments were inhabited by singles, once married and never married, with and without children. We sponsored a city-wide singles event and advertised it in all the singles publications. The event was a stand-up buffet, followed by dancing. From drawings for a door prize, we gathered names and addresses, which we added to our mailing list the next day. More than 350 singles attended the event, and several attended Sunday school the next morning. Since 1980, 40 percent of our new members have been single.

Growth Principle Sixteen: Growth Almost Always Occurs If the Congregation Is Friendly Toward Visitors.

Most churches think their greatest strength is their friendliness. What they usually mean is that the members are very friendly to one another. How they treat a visitor is another matter. Next Sunday, notice how the members of your church spend their free time before and after worship. Most will be huddled together in small groups, talking to one another, while visitors stand off by themselves looking lost. Being visitor-friendly doesn't just happen. It must be intentionalized through several actions on the part of the congregation.

Designate 5 percent of the budget for evangelism. If your church is filled with good people, and if your church has a people-centered ministry, let the public know. In the twentieth century, advertising is one way to follow our Lord's command that we not hide our light under a bushel. Jesus advertised when he preached the Sermon on the Mount on a mountainside, instead of in a river bed. Thirty-three percent of first-time visitors at Colonial Hills attend because of some form of advertising other than word of mouth!

When advertising, avoid small, cheap ads that simply invite people to your church; invite the unchurched to a specific event or highlight a specific need; use wording that is understandable to the unchurched; provide large, neat exterior signs; keep the grounds clean and inviting; use bright flowers; place the main exterior sign so it is visible from the most traveled road; pave and stripe all parking; in the Yellow Pages, place a large display ad that contains a logo of your church and a map showing how to get there; use as many listings as provided by your phone directory; place a regular ad that includes the church's logo on the church page of your newspapers; in other sections of the newspaper, run regular display ads that are different from the usual church ad.

A number of other ways to advertise your church's ministry exist, depending on the size of your church and the makeup of the community. The larger and more diverse the city, the more the following suggestions will benefit your church. Direct mail is more productive than door-to-door evangelism or flyers attached to doors, since it allows churches to target selected areas. The benefit of direct mail is cumulative, but it depends upon repetition. Mail to those areas from which most of the visitors attend, or concentrate on those areas from which few visitors attend. Concentrate the mailings at times when people are most likely to attend church—Christmas Eve, February through Easter, and June. Always invite people to a specific event, such as Vacation Bible School, Rally Sunday, major programs, or the opening of a new facility.

Radio offers an inexpensive way to target specific audiences. The best time to reach people by radio is when they are driving to and from work. Television is a key advertising factor for the large church, especially one in the downtown area. Colonial Hills found that people who attend because of television ads are more than twice as likely to join as those who attend for any other reason. There are three ways to use television: the broadcast of all or part of the worship service; thirty-second spots that offer a contemporary word several times a day; and talk shows that cover topics of interest outside the institutional or denominational realm.

Any declining downtown church with an endowment will do well to learn from the recent experiences of First United Methodist Church in Cleveland, Ohio. First Church had declined from 3,000 members to fewer than 200, with an average attendance of 57 in worship. When Kenneth Chalker became the pastor in 1986, his good instincts told him the church had great potential. Until that time, the church had used its endowment fund for all but $17,000 of the $320,000 budget. With Dr. Chalker's encouragement, the church agreed to use some of the endowment for an aggressive advertising program. After an intense search for the right firm, a program was developed to offer an authentic and effective invitation to the unchurched to attend worship at First Church.

The campaign consisted of print ads, direct mail, billboards on the sides of buses, and radio and television spots. As a result, worship attendance has increased to more than 300; 3,000 visitors have registered; 93 percent of the new members have joined by profession of faith; the Sunday school rolls have increased from 4 to 125; and the congregation has a renewed sense of hope and mission.

Contact visitors within twenty-four hours. The sooner visitors are personally contacted the more likely they are to join. On their way home from Sunday worship or lunch, members of Colonial Hills make what we call a Door-step Visit to all first-time visitors. During each service the color-coded visitor registration cards are compared with our visitors list, and each first-time visitor is taken a plant by one of the members. These plants are inexpensive ivies grown by members of our church. Visitors who are home are given the plant and thanked for caring enough to attend worship, but under no circumstances is the member to go into the house. If a visitor is not home, the plant is left on the doorstep with a note attached: "Welcome! From your friends at Colonial Hills United Methodist Church. We are so pleased we could worship together recently. May this plant remind you of the new life and growth that can occur as we are nurtured by God's love and the fellowship of his people. We look forward to worshiping together again soon."

Each visitor receives a phone call Sunday evening by either a paid or an unpaid staff member. A letter of welcome from the senior pastor is sent on Monday. The weekly newsletter arrives at the home on Thursday. The director of evangelism phones mid-week to set up an appointment to visit. If visitors return the following week, they are sent letters which include a list of the Sunday school classes, plus any information requested from previous contacts. A handwritten letter is sent after each personal visit, expressing pleasure over the visit and inviting the visitor to unite with our church. Before our next orientation class, a letter of invitation is sent, followed by a written invitation to unite. Follow-up phone calls by the pastors are made as needed. After three months, a letter is sent to those who have not returned, inviting them to join us again for worship. If they attend again, a letter is sent saying we are pleased to have them present again in worship, and the welcoming process begins again, except for the plant delivery.

The more contacts made, the more likely a family is to join. Don't be afraid to make repetitive calls on the same family. More families will respond favorably than will be turned off. A church 137 years old, Brentwood United Methodist Church in Brentwood, Tennessee,* believes in repetitive contact. Visitors who sign the register on Sunday are loaded into a computer and tracked. They receive four contacts the first week: They are called Sunday afternoon by a lay person; contacted by a "shepherd" in their geographic area, either in person or by phone; sent a letter from the pastor; and sent the church newsletter. If visitors return, the shepherds and staff work to get them into a Sunday school class or other group. The results—Brentwood has grown from 1,650 members to 3,036 in the last ten years.

Design the bulletin with both Joe and Max in mind. Most worship bulletins address the needs of Max, but few address the needs of Joe. Max appreciates ritual; Joe does not. Max knows the elements of worship; Joes does not. Max knows the names of the people involved in worship; Joe does not. Max knows people are welcome to join his church; Joe does not. Max doesn't mind if the service runs overtime; Joe does. Max knows how his church feels about visitors; Joe does not.

The worship bulletin portrays your congregation's attitude toward the visitor. If there is no mention in the bulletin about visitors, a subconscious message is sent to the visitor—we didn't plan for you to be here today. (See Chart 11 in the Appendix for a sample of the back page of our bulletin.)

Use every event in the life of the church as an entry point for membership. For example, at an Arts and Crafts Fair, have a drawing for some small item. To participate in the drawing, people need to fill out a slip with their name, address, and phone number. Add these names to your mailing list; invite them to your church; send them information about the church. Use the same procedure with your other events— an annual carnival, preschool, mothers' day out, Christmas Eve, Vacation Bible School, and all other such functions.

Put visitors on the mailing list the first time they visit. The most inexpensive form of communication and advertising is to send visitors a piece of mail from the church the same week they visit. If your newsletter is not mailed weekly, print extra copies and mail one to first-time visitors on Monday. A large mailing list should be a high priority. Help your secretary understand that there is a direct correlation between the size of the mailing list and the outreach ministry of the church. Weekly newsletters promote regular worship attendance.

Christmas Eve is a main entry point for the unchurched. The second most important day of the year for a church interested in reaching the unchurched is Christmas Eve (Stewardship Sunday is the first). Many of the families that attend worship Christmas Eve will join the church during the next year. Joe especially likes Christmas Eve, so it is an advantage to have several services. In 1988, Colonial Hills had five services on Christmas Eve.

Everything needs to be the best on Christmas Eve—the best music, the largest choir, the best sermon, the best service, and the finest decorations. Visitors should be welcomed, invited to join, and visited within the week. The services should not last much more than one hour. The bulletin should be written from the perspective of Joe and be the finest piece of printed material the church produces all year.

Provide adequate exterior and interior signs. The signs need to mark the restrooms, nursery, office, sanctuary, information booth, Sunday school classes, and special designated parking spaces. Signs should give directions the moment people drive onto the property.

Recently I experienced the aggravation first-time visitors feel when there are no signs to give them directions. I was conducting a church-growth seminar in a larger than average congregation. The Friday evening session went well, but on Saturday morning I arrived a few minutes early and the parking lot was empty. The front door I had used the night before was locked. So I waited. Ten minutes past the starting time, I walked around the building and found the group anxiously awaiting me. They had parked in a well-hidden lot at the back of the fellowship hall and had entered through a back door I knew nothing about. When I told the group what had happened, they were surprised to learn I did not know there was a back door. Max will usually assume that everyone knows what he knows about the church.

In determining the position and number of signs needed, work from the assumption that no one knows anything about your church. Ask visitors and new members to aid in the process. Consult with the custodian about the most-often-asked-for directions. Do not rely on Max to determine the need or place for signs.

From observing the way many churches treat their primary exterior sign, I offer the following suggestions: Face it toward the most traveled road adjacent to your property; make it as large as is appropriate; keep it neatly painted and in repair; make sure it is permanent and stable in appearance and reveals a high self-image within the congregation. Otherwise, take it down; it's bad advertising.

Provide separate registration cards for visitors and members. Use different colored forms and cards for visitors, so that it is easy to pick out the visitor cards from those of the members. On the visitors' registration forms, ask how they found your church and whether they desire a visit or an information packet. Also ask for family ages, address, telephone number, and comments on the visit to your church.

There are five disadvantages to the traditional registration pad that is passed from one worshiper to another: Not everyone registers at the same time; it is easier for Joe not to sign it if he is sitting toward the end of the pew; it discourages anyone from making serious comments to the pastor or suggestions about the church; it is harder for volunteers to use; it takes more time to track attendance, and it is harder to pick out and track visitors.

Visitor-friendly churches have an evangelism team. Colonial Hills has a full time director of evangelism who is expected to make ten to fifteen visits weekly in the homes of visitors, and at least fifteen hours of phone calls. It is also this person's responsibility to involve as many members as possible in evangelism.

Encouraging members to visit the unchurched is one of the most difficult forms of ministry. We gradually involve people through a four-step process. Our plant ministry, Door-step Visit, and greeter programs have provided easy entrance into the evangelism team. Every Sunday, more than 30 members are involved in these ministries. Next, we ask them to participate in our telemarketing ministry. Once a year, 100 members call 10,000 homes and develop a mailing list. We then invite the people on this list to some specific event at the church. From this, it is a much shorter step for our members to actually call at the home of a visitor.

There is growing evidence that baby boomers respond best to a telephone call, rather than a visit. The director of evangelism at Boston Avenue United Methodist Church in Tulsa, Oklahoma, Blaine Frierson, seldom makes home visits, and last year the church received some 370 new members. According to Reverend Frierson, "We use a home visit almost as a threat if they haven't joined." As of

1989, Colonial Hills uses only the phone with people between the ages of thirty and forty. Be alert to this new trend and monitor to find which works best in your area.

Designate 10 percent of your parking spaces for visitors. These spaces should be the closest to the sanctuary and marked Visitor Only. Signs should point visitors to these spaces as they enter the property. Parking attendants are helpful if a large part of the membership or community is elderly or if the parking is not close to the sanctuary.

Provide the members with plastic name tags (either clasps or pins). Name tags serve three purposes in a growing church: They help the pastor and members remember the growing list of new names; they tell the visitor which people are members; and they can be a signal to paid and unpaid staff that a person wishes to be recognized as a leader of the church. Ask new members which kind of name tag they would like. Mail all new members tags imprinted with their name and the name of the church. Provide a place in the foyer where the tags can be left before and after worship if desired.

Offer orientation classes for interested visitors. Colonial Hills offers an orientation class once each month during the main Sunday school hour. Because people join particular churches, rather than denominations, we give an overview of the Four Building Blocks of our church; explain that we expect members to take an active part in the ministry of the church, including a pledge; inform them how they can join; then answer any questions about our denomination. Since the class is not required for membership, it is open to visitors and recent new members. We feel we reach more people with this format than with a series of three or four sessions. The senior pastor needs to be part of this class.

Consider offering tours of the facilities following Sunday worship; membership Sundays for the shy or hesitant visitor; a coffee area in close proximity to the exit from worship; an information booth or designated area for information; and information packets. These packets could contain a generic brochure introducing your church, brochures on your various programs, a copy of the budget, a current calendar, a guide to the Sunday school, and an invitation to join.

Growth Principle Seventeen: Honestly Asking for Money Encourages Growth.

When people become honest with their money, the church grows! In 1979, Colonial Hills conducted a major capital fund drive that had many problems, and attendance at worship grew 15 percent. At the end of 1985, we made a passionate plea for additional funds to finish the year, and 1986 had the greatest worship increase to that date. Again in 1986, we needed a serious push to finish the year, and we experienced another large increase in worship attendance. And in 1987, in the midst of a depressed economy, we needed to raise $100,000 on Easter morning, just to be able to adopt a budget we had already lowered $193,000. And still we grew.

From 1969 until 1989, the budget of Colonial Hills grew from $14,000 to just under $1 million because we're clear about two things: We raise money to develop better stewards, rather than to meet a budget; and no apology should be given for trying to free people from their worship of money.

The best thing pastors can do for the people is to encourage them to be honest with their money. One-sixth of every word from our Lord is about money. He knows our basic sin—love of money.

Over the years, I've been impressed by the fact that 20 percent of the Christians I've known possess 80 percent of the enjoyment and satisfaction of being a Christian. Week after week, even during hard times, they live fulfilled lives. These people have discovered the Law of Congregational Life. They know they are healthiest when they reach out to help someone. And they apply this law to all areas of their life, even to the gain and use of their money. All are good stewards. I've never known a tither who did not know how to live. Pastors do the people an injustice when they fail to preach about the stewardship of money. So one of the best things a pastor can do for the members is to separate them from some of the money that stands between them and God.

Asking for money has not hurt the growth of Dayspring United Methodist Church.* Bert Lewis always talks about money for missions. His philosophy is that the more people give, the more they want to give, and the better they feel about giving. Over the last ten years, Dayspring's worship services have grown from 155 to 632, with a membership of only 900. Located in the southern section of Tempe, Arizona, near Arizona State University, Dayspring should grow. The interesting thing about this congregation is that its members are highly educated people, with an average age of 38. As a rule, this portion of our population has not learned the art of stewardship. But at Dayspring, because the pastor is not afraid to ask for money, the budget has grown from $67,924 to $565,000.

El Mesias United Methodist Church in Elgin, Illinois,* has an average pledge of $1,000, in a congregation where the average household income is $12,000 to $14,000. The members accomplished this by tithing. The church emphasizes spiritual growth, and as a result, in seven years has grown from 0 to 109 at worship, and 55 in Sunday school.

I've never seen a church that likes to talk about money. Either they don't understand the "people aspect" of money, or they know such talk hits them in the most unfaithful area of their lives. Breaking the grip money has on us is so difficult that money must be stressed as a separate category from all other forms of stewardship. Therefore, this section intentionally refers to *pledging* instead of *stewardship*. We know that stewardship, like evangelism, is involved in all that we are. But we've learned that like evangelism, when stewardship is thought of as a part of our whole ministry, it becomes nobody's job.

Do not ask people to give to the church or tell them the church needs their money. Ask people to give to *God*, rather than to a church or a budget. We have a need to give, and we will not find fulfillment until we learn to give out of all that we have. As we reach out to help others, we are helped.

Have the pledge drive first, then set the budget. In that way, it is easier for members to understand that they are not supporting a budget, but are giving because that's what God intends for them to do. It is okay to ask for more money until every person in the congregation is tithing. It is better to encourage people to tithe or give on a percentage basis than to ask them to give to a budget.

Never calculate and publicize how easy the budget would be met if every member of the congregation gave an average gift of so many dollars. That only encourages average giving from those who might become tithers.

One of the finest stewardship programs for small and medium churches is the "Sunday Consecration Steward-ship Program" by Herb Miller. The entire program is based on the need of the person to give, rather than on the need of the church to raise a budget. Each person is encouraged to start where he or she is and step up toward tithing. This program has been used widely throughout the United States to help churches develop biblical stewards, instead of merely raising budgets. According to Miller, the program "virtually always gets a 20%, frequently 30%, occasionally 40% increase in giving the first year." (Contact Net Press, 5001 Avenue N, Lubbock TX 79412. Tel. 1-800-638-3463.)

First United Methodist Church in Spring Hills, Florida, is an example of the many success stories of churches that use a modified version of Herb Miller's program. The church's budget grew from $249,000 in 1987 to $370,000 in 1989.

Pledge Sunday is the most important day of the year. Few churches understand the importance of both the pledge drive and the particular day it is celebrated in worship. Set aside at least six weeks to build toward Pledge Sunday. Do not attempt to ask for pledges without three to four weeks of prior education in Sunday school, through the newsletter, direct mailings to the congregation, and lay speakers from the pulpit. Involve at least one-fourth of your worshiping congregation in the preparation for Pledge Sunday. This involvement is the most important aspect of a pledge drive. Do not allow any program to detract either from the drive or from the leaders' energy.

Pledge drives are most effective on an annual basis because of inflation, the mobility of the congregation, the influx of new members, and the fast pace of change in our world. It is even debatable whether building fund drives should last longer than two years. In a few years, it may be necessary for churches to have semiannual stewardship drives.

One of the best times to conduct a pledge drive is between February and Mothers' Day. We moved from a fall to a spring pledge drive in 1986, and that year our pledge totals jumped more than 35 percent! Why? More people are present in worship during this period than at any other time of the year. Spring brings new hope and excitement, and Christmas bills have been paid in most pledging households. Separating the financial year from the calendar year creates two major periods when people are made aware of the need to take care of their pledge.

Designate one percent of the general budget for educating the people to be better stewards of their wealth. It takes money to develop stewards. Often it is best to hire someone for a month to oversee the logistics of the program. This person must be superorganized and not afraid to ask others for help; it does not matter whether he or she has expertise in financial matters. All materials should be of the best quality, but most of the expenses of the pledge program at Colonial Hills are for two catered meals—one for the workers and one for the congregation. Covered-dish suppers are usually ineffective and work against the desired results in churches that have more than 150 at worship services.

Pledge cards should ask only for money. Time and talent commitments should *not* be part of the pledge drive, since such attempts usually result in less commitment of money. Stewardship of time and talent should be asked for each year, but at a separate time—perhaps three months prior to the pledge drive.

The pastor must take the lead in the pledge drive. Pastors should make public statements about the specifics of their giving; encourage members to increase their giving by one percent of their annual income, if they are not already tithing; preach at least two sermons on Christians' need to give; and be involved in setting the priorities of the budget.

The pastor needs to know how much each person gives. There is no difference between knowing how often members attend worship and give of their time and talent, and knowing how they give of their wealth. There appears to be a difference only because for most of us, money is our God, and we don't want others to know how self-centered we are.

Budgets of growing churches should never be more than 70 to 90 percent underwritten by pledges. If the entire budget is underwritten by a pledge drive, increase it immediately. If a growing church underwrites its whole budget through pledges, it says to the congregation one of three things: (1) We do not expect to receive any new members, and if we do, we do not expect them to be good stewards; (2) we do not want any new members; or (3) if we receive any new members, we do not plan to add the necessary space to accommodate them.

There is a way to arrive at a challenging, yet safe level for your budget. Based on your past experience, estimate how many new members you expect will join during the next year. Then, based on past giving records of new members, determine the approximate amount the new members will give during the year. Divide this amount by one-half, since some will join early in the year; others, late. Add this amount to the pledges, along with other historically documented monies you expect to receive, such as endowments, building-usage fees, special offerings that go toward the general budget, loose-plate offerings, identified nonpledgers, and fund raisers. The total is a fair estimate of expected income based on present giving patterns.

Select unpaid pledge-drive leaders on the basis of their giving patterns and their willingness to give of themselves to others. It is the pastor's role to make sure that the elected leadership of the church is leading the church in all areas of stewardship, including wealth. It doesn't matter whether these leaders have financial expertise, only that they have the respect of the congregation and are leaders in the art of giving—not that their pledges are the largest, but that they represent *sacrificial* giving. Often small pledges represent more of a tithe than do large pledges. God will not honor a stewardship program in which the leaders are not setting the standard.

Contact each new member to secure a pledge. Mail a pledge card to all new members the second week after they join, accompanied by a self-addressed stamped envelope and a letter asking that the card be returned within the week. If the card is not returned within thirty days, a member of the Stewardship Committee should attempt to obtain a pledge over the phone. Not contacting new members for a pledge is telling them that their money is not needed, or that their joining went unnoticed.

Keep detailed records of giving and pledge patterns. The Ministry Audit in chapter 7 will show the kind of record keeping necessary for accurate evaluation and projection. These records serve to identify windows of opportunity and red flag problems. Six areas of the budget are most important to track: salaries, debt service, program, advertising, pledge drive, and outreach.

Vary the stewardship emphasis and target portions of the congregation. Three groups of members should be targeted on a rotating basis—pledgers, nonpledgers, and big pledgers. The objective is that all members become tithers, but the steps to reach that objective are different for each member.

During one year, target the nongivers. The primary objective here is to broaden the pledge base by starting more members on the road to tithing. Ask these members to begin making a regular commitment. The following year, ask them to step up to tithing by giving one percent of their income.

Another year, target the large givers. Tell them they are the major contributors to the church and that much is expected of them. Also target families that *could* be large givers.

In still another year, target the large portion of the congregation that gives but does not tithe. Ask these people to step up to tithing by giving one percent more. Each stewardship program should clearly target one of these three categories and build a strategy around it.

Encourage designated giving; discourage unified budgets. People born before World War II usually prefer for the church to decide how to spend their money, whereas people born after World War II prefer to have a voice in how their money is spent. Let your pledge card appeal to both by providing a place for giving to the general budget as well as several opportunities for designated giving (see Chart 12 in the Appendix for a sample pledge card).

People who respond best to this type of pledge card are members born after World War II; newer members who have not yet become people like Max; members who give under five dollars a week; members who have a driving passion for a particular outreach ministry of the church; members born before World War II who want their money to go just to the building fund; college graduates under thirty-five who are suspicious of the institutional church. Stewardship committees need to understand that people give for different reasons.

People give to help people rather than to goals or programs. Personalize your approach in every way possible. Make pictures, not figures, prominent in your brochures. Use pictures of respected key leaders. Talk in terms of people, not budgets or ideas. Show how the money will meet physical and spiritual needs. Choose leaders for the pledge campaign who are respected and work well with others.

In 1988, the widower of a prominent leader in our church was asked to be one of the stewardship-drive speakers during worship. In essence, he said, "I never understood why my wife insisted on tithing until she died. Now I do. The discipline of tithing taught her how to live and to die."

Encourage regular special offerings throughout the year. Depending on the intensity of the drives, a growing church can benefit from six to twelve special offerings a year. At least half of these offerings should be designated for already budgeted items. The offerings should vary in their appeal. Max is loyal to the church and will give out of commitment and duty. But Joe will give out of compassion. Don't be afraid to have two or three offerings a year for the budget, in addition to the pledge drive. Special offerings on the first Sunday of the month are always more successful. The last Sunday of the month is the worst Sunday to have a special offering.

Christmas is usually the best time to raise money for your church's budget. The Christmas offering at Colonial Hills equals almost three-quarters of an additional month's income. In 1987, against a budget income of $843,000, our Christmas offering was over $50,000. In 1988, against a budget income of $943,000, our Christmas offering was close to $50,000. We begin taking the Christmas offering on the first Sunday in December and continue through the month, including Christmas Eve. We always designate the money for one of our budget's outreach ministries—one that appeals to the congregation. Don't low-key the Christmas offering or set too low a goal. And don't designate it for some denominational ministry outside the budget. Doing so will drastically lower the offering. Take denominational offerings at other times; you'll raise the same amount of money. Members will give much more at Christmas if the offering goes for a budgeted mission for which they are passionately concerned.

Easter also is a good time to have special offerings. An excellent program is one called Thirty Pieces of Silver. Place a silver dollar in a purple bag and send one to every family in the church the week of Ash Wednesday. Ask each family to put another silver dollar aside every day during Lent.

On either Palm Sunday or Easter, ask the members and visitors to bring their offering to the altar—a gesture to turn the betrayal-price of Christ into an offering of love.

An increase in worship attendance results in an increase in giving. Income toward the budget in a healthy church should exceed $1,000 for every person in attendance at an average Sunday worship service. If your church has 200 in worship, your income toward the budget should be over $200,000, not including foundation money or borrowed funds. The location of the church, or its affluence or lack thereof, seldom has much bearing on the amount of income.

The more balanced the spread of income, the healthier a church will be. It is best if one-third of the congregation gives no more than half of the church's income. When one-third contributes more than two-thirds, broaden the base of congregational support to avoid concentrating both the power and the future of the church in too few families.

Keep your debt service under 30 percent of your total operating and building budget. A growing church should not allow its debt service to exceed more than 33 percent of its budget for more than two years. Twenty-eight percent is the amount many lending institutions consider maximum. There is a difference between debt service and debt. *Debt* is the amount of money owed. *Debt service* is the amount paid on the debt each year. In determining how much debt a church can afford, it is best to talk in terms of debt service, rather than debt. The amount a church can afford is affected too much by changing interest rates and the length of the loan for the debt itself to be the determining factor.

Always be in debt to something—either mortgages or missions. Never burn a mortgage note without first designating the freed-up money for some new specific ministry or mission. Not to do so is a signal to the congregation that its money is not needed as much next year.

Churches are not in the business of saving money and drawing interest at the bank. It is not good to have a lot of money in the bank unless it is in the form of a foundation, with the principal and interest designated and used regularly for some outreach ministry. In this way, the congregation will not begin to rely on it for daily existence. Money in the bank for which there is no definite need is a deterrent to the development of good stewards; it teaches people that their money is not needed.

Avoid the use of plaques. Plaques will raise money, but they do not lend to the glory of God or to easy movement from one building or site to another. Plaques often allow one or two families to gain too much recognition and thereby too much control of the decision-making process. Colonial Hills could have raised more money several times if we had allowed plaques.

Avoid cutting the budget! Instead of cutting, look for additional ways to raise funds. If the budget must be cut, have a special offering to take up the slack. The role of the finance committee should be to find ways to raise money instead of tracking how money is spent. A think-tank session is more productive than simply a review of financial statements. Budgets should be increased by at least the average inflation of the community's income.

In 1987, because of the Texas economy, we had to cut our budget for the first time in nineteen years, from a projected need of $989,000 to $793,000! The 1986 budget had been $893,000. The only way we could meet that budget was to raise $100,000 that same month, so that the actual budget for the new year would be the same as the one for the previous year. We did that, and the point was made—it is costly to cut a budget. But by the next year our budget was back to $943,000.

Growth Principle Eighteen: Long-term Growth Needs a Solid Foundation.

This foundation may include having and consistently using an overall vision, mission statement, logo, song, yearly updated five- or ten-year plan, adopted objectives, master plan for use of land and facilities, and clarity about the church's major weaknesses and strengths.

An overall vision for a congregation is the most important aspect of a solid foundation. Think of vision in terms of a destination your church needs to arrive at in the future. A church needs to know where God wants it to go so that it will know if and when it gets there. Visions are never measurable and are therefore distinguishable from objectives, which are always measurable. Visions are more conceptual and form the basis for strategies or objectives. It is from such a vision that mission statements are developed.

A mission statement helps a church focus its preparation of budget and ministry, and sets the context in which objectives can be set. The statement needs to be clear, measurable, unlimiting and, if possible, short enough to commit to memory so it can be used in worship services.

A church logo helps give identity and public recognition to the congregation. If a church develops a logo, it should be used on every piece of printed material given to the public. The color and shape should remain the same.

Church songs are helpful but not vital. If a church has a song, it should be one that is usable in worship on a regular basis. Many churches commission someone to compose anthems for their church.

Regularly updated five- or ten-year plans are vital. A long-term plan does three things: It helps leaders evaluate and better understand the congregation; it gives the pastor and members a framework in which to decide whether this is the church in which they wish to spend their future years; it helps eliminate surprises and facilitates quicker response to growth.

The larger the congregation, the more input and initiative is expected from the staff in formulating a long-term plan. Church leaders need to realize that very few members want input into the direction of the church's ministry, as long as it meets their own needs. But whatever the size of the church,

the more members involved in developing a long-term
plan, the better the plan will be.

At Frazer Memorial UMC, long-range planning is done
by the Joel Committee. Every two years, a committee of
twenty to twenty-five members, chaired by the pastor, is
given the responsibility of "dreaming God's dream for
Frazer." John Ed Mathison gives the committee members
advance assignments and materials, so that when they
meet they have a framework from which to start. The Joel
Committee then updates projections, identifies needs, and
makes broad-stroke recommendations, which are referred
to the appropriate committees or task forces for detailing
and implementation. Half the people are on the committee
by virtue of holding an office; the other half represent
different interests throughout the church.

The danger of long-term plans is that some members
consider such plans to be set in concrete rather than in
process. Any plan should be just that—a plan. A plan is a
process that can and should be changed on the basis of the
needs of people and the ability of the congregation to
respond.

*Develop a master plan for the use of all available land and
facilities.* Master plans are best developed around the
following questions: What is the relationship between the
number of cars that can be parked, the number of buildings
that can be built, and the number of people that can be
served? What are the objectives of the church? How much
land is available? What is the desired environment? What is
the financial ability of the congregation? A master plan
should be the first mission attempted by a new congregation, and it should show how large the church can grow on
that site.

Know your church's major strengths and weaknesses. Concentrate and build on your church's strengths. This does
not mean that churches should ignore their weaknesses,
especially if those weaknesses are so acute that they
jeopardize the ability of the church to meet the spiritual and

physical needs of people. Weaknesses should be addressed, but not as intensely as you address your strengths.

Growth Principle Nineteen: Regular Strategic Planning Is Necessary for Healthy Growth

---

The Greek word for strategy, *strategia*, refers to the plan of a general who has set up camp on a hill overlooking the battlefield. The idea is that the general has a vantage point from which to see the big picture. As the battle is waged, the general moves the soldiers and equipment in order to win the battle; but if necessary, he is willing to sacrifice some aspects of the battle to win the war.

The Church of Jesus Christ is engaged in a battle for the souls of humankind. Every church needs the kind of leadership that can see the big picture, consider the options, and make the strategic decisions that win the war. The smaller the congregation, the more this leadership is vested

Figure 6: Rolling Model

in the pastor. The larger the congregation, the more it is vested in the pastor and paid staff.

The Rolling Model seen in Figure 6 is an excellent tool for short- and long-term strategic planning. The center of the wheel is the overriding vision of a church. If the vision isn't in place, nothing else works well. The five sections represent the skills needed to implement the vision, as well as the excuses people will give to maintain the status quo. While very few people have all five skills, most people have at least one. The model is in the form of a wheel because strategic planning is always a process that moves toward a destination. The processes represented in this wheel are thought, time, energy, skill, sequence, people, purpose, growth, and importance.

The Rolling Model asks six basic questions: Where does God want this church to go? What commitment must we make now to insure that we will move toward our destination? How do we get to our destination? Who can best get us there? When do we start? Did we reach our destination; was it worth the trip?

Vision: Where does God want our church to go? If a solid foundation has been laid, a congregation will have an overall vision as to where the church is going and what it will be like. All strategic planning begins here. The vision of Colonial Hills is to have a healthy church that nurtures its members and reaches the unchurched, as defined in the Four Building Blocks.

A classic example of a new church becoming a large church because of vision is St. James United Methodist Church in Little Rock, Arkansas. St. James planned from the beginning to be a large church. In 1969, a small group of 40 charter members had a vision of a 4,000-member church. Acting upon this vision, they sold the smaller plot given to them by the denomination and purchased seven acres. They then asked an architect to draw up a site master plan, showing the utilization of the acres. Upon the arrival in 1976 of the present pastor, John Miles, another three acres were purchased. To date, they have built six of the seven buildings planned in 1969. St. James had grown from an average worship attendance of 106 to 1,112 in 1987.

St. James does have one major problem. It is short about 200 parking spaces. That may be one of the reasons worship attendance declined from a high of 1,310 in 1986. How St. James cures its parking needs may determine much of its future.

Strategy: What must we commit to now, to insure that we will arrive at our destination? The most difficult part of strategic planning is deciding *what* we must commit to *now* to insure the future. People tend to become sidetracked by the details of *how, who, when,* and *why,* and never commit to a strategy of *what* must be done *now,* no matter what the obstacle. The *what* question of strategic planning has nothing to do with details. Details can overwhelm people who are not already committed to a basic strategy. The *what* question sets the objectives.

Leadership by objective, or goal setting, looks at the present situation in light of the overall vision of the church, and decides *what* we must commit to *now* so that the future will be influenced by our vision. Unlike the vision, objectives will change as situations change. But once a congregation decides *what* it must commit to *now* to move toward the vision, nothing must get in the way of achieving that vision.

Objectives need to be people-centered and measurable. People-centered objectives help churches manage, celebrate, and plan their growth; make it possible for church leaders, rather than the situation, to determine the church's future; help congregations guard against Christian nurture taking a back seat to numerical growth; and keep outreach from suffering due to a growing indebtedness.

Measurable objectives encourage churches to celebrate when the objective is reached; raise the morale of the congregation and encourage faith in the future; help the pastor and congregation understand each other's value systems; and help the pastor and congregation priortize their activities. The use of long-term personal objectives is one way to foster longer pastoral tenures.

An example of allowing a church's vision to determine objectives occurred at Colonial Hills in response to the 1987 economic downturn in Texas. Two years prior to the downturn, we had purchased $1 million worth of additional land, with no payments for eighteen months. At the height of the economic downturn it was time to begin paying on the land. This caused postponement of additional staff, facilities, and outreach ministries, all of which were needed if we were to continue to meet the spiritual and physical needs of others. In response to this situation we decided to commit ourselves to an eighteen-month strategy (see Chart 13 in the Appendix). The plan included six short-term and three long-term objectives.

The short-term objectives were to reach an average attendance of one person in the 11:00 chancel choir for every ten people in each worship service by December 1987; to discontinue all meetings except the administrative board and the executive committee and, in their place, conduct a series of congregational parties in members' homes; to give top priority in 1988 to restoring our outreach giving to its level in 1987 before the impact of the Texas economy; after paying apportionments, to reestablish the television ministry before any other outreach ministry; to raise a minimum of $100,000 on Easter of 1987, in order to continue the basic ministries of our church during this eighteen-month period; to move the five-year plan forward eighteen months.

The long-term objectives were to bring present staff salaries up to a competitive level with churches of comparable size before adding additional paid staff; to increase worship attendance to an average of 1,000; to be sure our debt service returned to less than 30 percent of the total budget before we increased our $2.2 million indebtedness. *Long term* was understood to mean between eighteen months and three years.

The combination of these objectives forced the congregation to reach out to both the spiritual and the physical needs of others during the eighteen-month period. The adoption of these objectives declared that we, not the situation, would shape our future. The objectives were measurable enough for us to know whether we could celebrate their achievement. And they allowed the pastor and congregation to plan for the future and prioritize their daily ministries.

In order to show how strategic planning works, we will follow the worship-attendance objective through the various steps of the Rolling Model.

Tactical: How do we get to our destination? Often objectives are never reached because the details of implementing them are not well defined and given top priority. Every objective should have a checklist that is followed meticulously. This list should include such items as advertising, staging, equipment, facilities, setting, child care, and personnel. Never assume anything about details.

In order to reach our objective of 1,000 in worship, we developed the following tactical How list: Insure that the crib and toddler nursery can handle a 20 percent increase; remodel the sanctuary so that the choir has room to grow to an average attendance of 50; select thirty ministries of our church to be highlighted on particular Sundays, and give a special invitation to those people targeted to be in worship; design and erect a new church sign; step up our advertising campaign by $10,000; highlight our music ministry and the choice of two preachers on Sunday; send six direct mailings to 10,000 homes, giving an invitation to a special event; insure that no retreats last through Sunday; expand our foyer to be able to handle the flow of an additional 150 people; double the number of ushers and greeters; increase the number of bulletins printed each week; restructure

Communion so that it will not take excessively long with the additional people; add a fourth and a fifth Christmas Eve service; begin a search for an additional associate pastor; make room for 100 more people in our already crowded Sunday school; begin groundwork for the establishment of a building committee for the Sunday after Easter 1988; decide by May 1988 on the date of the next building fund drive; encourage adult choirs to present three cantatas each year; discontinue the practice of adult choirs taking a month off during the summer; rehearse all special worship services; monitor our parking to insure that it remains under 80-percent capacity—discuss the implications if it does not; increase the salary of the director of music ministry by a suggested substantial amount; establish one new outreach ministry in 1988; develop our foundation to $1 million by 1995.

Much of this strategy may appear too costly. Our members felt so at first, but we decided we could not afford not to do the plan, so we borrowed the necessary money. Church growth, like grace, is costly. Not to take action is always more expensive in the long run.

Delegation: Who can best get us to our destination? Delegation is the careful selection of people whose skills are matched to the tasks. In selecting leadership, remember that very few people have all the skills listed in the Rolling Model. Some people are good at thinking strategically, but poor at implementing a plan, no matter how well the plan is detailed. Prior to your selection, provide a job description that spells out the minimum requirements to effectively accomplish the objective. Then hold the people accountable for whatever has been delegated to them. Publicize the people who are in charge of each task or program. Check back at regular intervals, and be available to those to whom you have delegated the tasks.

In implementing our worship objective, responsibility was delegated to several people. The director of music ministry needed to make sure the ratio of one-to-ten was a priority for the adult choirs. A Futures Committee was chosen to determine what the church needed to do in order to provide the space for worship to continue to grow. The preaching pastors must continue to give their best in sermon preparation. The director of evangelism needed to broaden the base of lay participation in evangelism. And a building committee must select architects and supervise any building projects.

Most denominations do not provide an organizational structure that includes a committee to do strategic planning. For that reason, Colonial Hills has a Futures Committee. The people on this committee are chosen on the basis of their ability to see the overall picture or vision. (An example of the committee's work can be seen in the Appendix, Chart 14.)

Implementation: When do we start? Often the success of an objective will depend upon the numerous details falling into place in a certain sequence. In planning the worship campaign, we arrived at the following time sequence: (1) Remodel the sanctuary and expand the narthex by Easter 1987; (2) add to adult choir to reach a 45 average at 11:00 worship by December 1988; (3) design a new sign by January 1988 and erect it before Easter 1988; (4) step up our advertising and bulk mailings during the fall of 1987; (5) review educational space in fall of 1987 and make full use of all space by January 1988; (6) have three cantatas each year and end vacation for choir in 1987; (7) restructure Communion before Christmas Eve 1987; (8) add the fourth Christmas Eve service by September 1987, the fifth by September 1988; (9) expand the number of bulletins as needed; (10) select a Futures Committee in 1988; (11) have a capital fund drive in the fall of 1987 or 1988.

Evaluation: Did we reach our destination, and was it worth the effort? Regular evaluations force us to see our mistakes and our successes; help us learn to apply these mistakes and successes to new and similar situations; tell us whether the event met the objective and whether we can do it again.

If the plan was for a short period of time, evaluate it as

soon as possible. List the strengths and weaknesses. Be brutal and thorough. Ask, Did it achieve the objective? Was it worth the effort and money? Is it worth doing again? What are its implications for our total ministry?

If the plan covers an extended period of time, evaluate each step to see whether corrections need to be made or other tactics employed to insure the success of the objective. Ask the same questions asked for short-term plans. Because our worship campaign objective covered a three-year period, we evaluated each step. We are presently two years into our plan, and we have evaluated according to the following:

We will need six months more recovery than we had anticipated. However, worship has increased from 683 in 1985 to more than 900 in 1989. The 11:00 service averages 20 people short of 80 percent. The foyer addition in 1987 is allowing better flow and fellowship. The choir rehearsal space was a major drawback to more growth, so we moved the choir room and expanded it in January 1988. Moving the choir, eliminating the summer vacation, and encouraging three cantatas a year resulted in a 59 percent increase in the 11:00 adult choir, but having two adult choirs is a deterrent to reaching our objective of one choir member for every ten people in the service. The director of music ministry's salary was increased as suggested. Rearranging our educational space has helped with the overcrowded conditions. But for growth to continue, we needed more space, so we added a three-room portable in 1988, and we still will need an additional 20,000 square feet over the next five years.

Based on this evaluation, in January 1989 the Futures Committee recommended in $2 million capital fund drive to raise a portion of the money needed to build a 1,200-seat sanctuary and a 20,000-square foot educational building. The report was unanimously adopted and is now being implemented. A building committee has been established, and architects and fund raisers have been hired.

Growth Principle Twenty: It Takes More Effort to Implement Change Than to Maintain the Status Quo or Exercise Veto Power.

Strategic planning needs constant reinforcement, so that one or two key members of a church who do not agree with the vision or the objectives arrived at by the majority do not slow down or stop the process.

Tom McClung, pastor of Windcrest United Methodist Church in San Antonio, Texas, shares his insight on this principle:

My experience at Windcrest certainly supports Growth Principle Twenty. At the time of your seminar with us, we were the third-fastest-growing church in our Conference over the last twenty years. At the advice of two consultants, we decided to build a larger sanctuary. Our 11:00 A.M. service had been over 80 percent full for two years, and the 9:30 A.M. service was nearly half full.

At each of the decision points, the vote to move forward required new energies, such as a seminar on sanctuary planning; special offering for the architectural fees for the design phase; additional fund raising, research, and planning for working drawings and specifications; choosing a bond program to finance the project; selection of a consultant for a three-year pledge campaign for a capital funds drive; approval of plans and placing the project for bids; heavy congregational involvement in the sale of bonds; and numerous meetings to make building decisions.

In addition, there is the psychological and spiritual effort on the part of the pastor to make peace with the inevitable conflict about what kind or size church we should be. The abrasions of our fast-changing situation have called me to firm up my strength of independence. It has been especially important to resist my temptation to allow others to tell me who I am. A sense of identity as a servant of the Good Shepherd who seeks and saves the lost is essential. . . .

The energy expended by the pastor for growth is second

only to the effort devoured by the demoralization and
despair of a dying church which refuses to face the realities
of its situation. Any pastor or lay person who wants to be
part of a growing church should be prepared for some good
old-fashioned hard work!

Three great sins exist in most mainline Protestant churches.
One, we are more concerned about being nice than with
being Christian. Church members have been taught that it
is better to be nice to one another than faithful to their
convictions. What we don't realize is that in worrying about
not offending a few people, we don't reach out to the many
unchurched who live within the shadow of our church.

Two, we are more in love with fear than with Christ. Fear
of failure, of not being accepted, of losing control of our
church, and fear of change have such a firm grip on our lives
that we are afraid to take any kind of action. So we just react
to life rather than taking action to improve it. Many
long-term members simply do not want to share power
with newcomers.

Three, we care more about tradition than about mission.
What has happened to us in the past is more important than
what can happen to us in the future. We have allowed
circumstances and events to stifle and derail our mission in
life as a church.

These three sins must be acknowledged, forgiven, and
eliminated from our actions in order for mainline Protestants to once again strategically meet the physical and
spiritual needs of society. Pastors and laity must covenant
together to pray and work for the removal of those sins from
the life of our churches.

Conclusion

Here are four words of caution to those interested in
strategic planning. One, begin the process only if members
of the paid and unpaid staff are willing to pay the price of
hard work and sacrifice. Two, in forming the vision or in

setting the objectives, decide on *what* has to be done *now* in order for your church's vision to be a reality, before discussing the details or the logistics of how to accomplish those objectives. Three, give more attention to the majority who wish to implement change than to the few who wish to exercise their veto power. Four, before attempting any of the above, ask God for guidance.

Apply these four cautions to the strategic-planning process outlined in this chapter, and your church will be not only healthier, but better able to meet the spiritual and physical needs of God's people.

You are now ready to collect the material asked for in the Ministry Audit in order to evaluate the windows of opportunity and red-flag the challenges facing your church. In doing so, your church can experience growth with biblical integrity.

CHAPTER SEVEN

The Ministry Audit

THE MINISTRY AUDIT HAS BEEN SHARED WITH MORE THAN 500 PASTORS IN 44 STATES DURING THE LAST THREE years, in churches ranging in size from newly established to memberships of 3,300. In each instance the results have been that problems are red-flagged, windows of opportunity are recognized before they close, and strategies are developed to address the challenges.

Go through each section of the audit to determine whether its use could be of major benefit to your church. If the decision is Yes, ask the church to authorize either a standing committee or a special task force on strategic planning to read this book and complete the Ministry Audit.

You will need to gather the necessary data from three sources. First, conduct a survey in worship services for four consecutive weeks, avoiding holidays or special Sundays (see Chart 1 in the Appendix). This survey can be done before, during, or after the collection of other data.

Second, gather from the church files all the historical, financial, and factual material. Be very careful that this information is accurate.

Third, ask the elected leaders of your church to answer those questions in the audit marked with an asterisk. It is helpful if each person has read this book.

Then compile all the information into the Ministry

Audit. The audit is divided into four sections that correspond to the Four Building Blocks. Where needed, forms and directions are included. When you finish gathering the material for each section, write in your own conclusions.

Do not take action on any section of the Ministry Audit until the entire audit is finished. It may be of benefit to refer the findings of each section to an appropriate standing committee for consideration, but the church should not be asked to respond to this study until the audit is completely finished.

One month should be sufficient for completing the audit. The audit follows closely with the material in each chapter. *The questions marked with an asterisk should be answered by the elected officials of the church.*

All Ministry Must Be People-centered.

Growth Principle One: Growth Is Not Concerned with Numbers, But with Meeting the Needs of People.

YES / NO

1. When we design programs, do we first consider the individual needs of the membership? _____

2. Do we make our members feel guilty by telling them their church needs them to take part in various programs or events?* _____

3. Does our church encourage the members to say what they need from the church?* _____

4. Does our congregation design its own programs to fit its particular needs, rather than using denominational or generic programs? _____

5. What is the age, sex, and marital status of adult worshipers? (give % of each)

18–19 ____ %	20–34 ____ %	35–49 ____ %	50+ ____ %
M/M _____	M/M _____	M/M _____	M/M _____	M = __ %
M/S _____	M/S _____	M/S _____	M/S _____	F = __ %
F/M _____	F/M _____	F/M _____	F/M _____	Mar = __ %
F/S _____	F/S _____	F/S _____	F/S _____	Sgl = __ %

6. How do our answers for Question 5 compare to the statistics for our area? Contact the Chamber of Commerce for this information:

   18–19 ____ %   20–34 ____ %   35–49 ____ %   50+ ____ %

   Based on this comparison, what age group
   do we need to concentrate on?   _____

7. Which methods should we use in discovering the individual needs of the congregation?

   One to One   _____

   Specific programs   _____

   Small groups   _____

   Combination of the above   _____

8. Does our pastor understand the everyday
   world of our members?*   _____

9. What are our people programs—including specialized ministries?

   _____

   _____

   _____

10. Does our church act as if people are more
    important than rules?*   _____

11. Are our relationships more important than
    our doctrine?*   _____

12. Has there been any major controversy or division in the last five years? If so, what was it?

    _____

    _____

13. Does our church deal openly with contro-
    versy?*   _____
14. What is our decision-making process?

_____

_____

_____

15. Do our boards or committees consider the
    psychological needs of those who attend?   _____
16. Do our board and committee members understand the
    difference between a working board and
    an information board?*   _____
17. If our board consists of more than 25 people, do we have an
    official executive committee to do the basic
    work?   _____
18. Can ministry decisions be made quickly,
    without a lot of red tape?*   _____
19. Can new members be added to committees
    and boards without major delay?*   _____
20. Do we make most of our ministry decisions
    with reference to church polity or policy?*   _____
21. Is any manner of dress welcome at worship
    and at board or committee meetings?*   _____
22. Is it likely that a new member could become
    chairperson of a board in less than a year?*   _____
23. What is the ratio of program money to total
    budget?   _____

    Is it 10%?   _____
24. Who gives or withholds permission for new ideas or ministries
    in our church?

_____

25. Do we encourage meetings that last less
    than an hour?   _____
26. What do we do to nurture ex-leaders?

_____

_____

27. Does our church have a positive image in
the community?*   _____
28. What is our church known for on the community grapevine?*

_____

_____

29. Do we know what the community is saying
about us?*   _____
30. Do we respond to what is being said about
us?*   _____
31. Conclusion: _____

_____

_____

_____

Growth Principle Two: Growth Occurs When People Are
Given a Wide Variety of Choices.

1. Is our church willing to allow into our membership people
who express their faith differently from the
way we do?*   _____
2. Do we encourage people to develop their
faith according to their own needs?*   _____
3. Does our church offer a balanced ministry? List our various
programs under the following headings:

Love   Justice   Mercy
(Nurture)   (Social Action)   (Evangelism)

_____

_____

_____

4. Does our church offer more than one Sunday
morning worship service?   _____
What hours?   _____
5. If more than one, does the same pastor
preach each service?   _____
6. Once we start a new service of worship, are
we willing to continue it?   _____

 7. Are we willing to have a worship service at
    the same time as Sunday school?   _____

 8. Does our church have a pre-school?   _____
    How many attend?   _____

 9. Does our church have a grade school?   _____
    How many attend?   _____

10. Does our church have a mothers' day out?   _____

11. Do we start a new Sunday school class every
    three to six months?   _____

12. Number of adult Sunday school classes: _____
    How many attend?   _____

13. Number of singles Sunday school classes: _____
    How many attend?   _____

14. Number of youth Sunday school classes: _____
    How many attend?   _____

15. Number of children's Sunday school
    classes: _____
    How many attend?   _____

16. When was the last adult Sunday school class
    started?   _____

17. Does our church have Sunday evening programs?

    _____

18. Does our church have mid-week programs?

    _____

19. Does our church have Bible studies?

    _____

20. Does our church have athletic programs?

    _____

21. Other: _____

22. Conclusion:

    _____

    _____

Growth Principle Three: Growth Occurs When People Are Matched with Their Skills.

1. What is our nominating process?

_____

2. Is our nominating process tailored to fit our
   congregation?   _____

3. Do we choose our leaders carefully, without
   making blanket appeals for volunteers?   _____

4. Do we nominate people only to positions
   which have a definite task to perform?   _____

5. Conclusion: _____

_____

_____

Growth Principle Four: Growth Does Not Dictate That More People Will Become Inactive.

1. List membership figures for last 10 years (most recent year first).

   _____   _____   _____

   _____   _____   _____

   _____   _____   _____

                                              _____

2. List membership losses for last ten years (most recent year first).

Death	Withdrawal	UM Transfers	OD Transfers	=	Total
_____	_____	_____	_____		_____
_____	_____	_____	_____		_____
_____	_____	_____	_____		_____

_____ _____ _____ _____ _____

_____ _____ _____ _____ _____

_____ _____ _____ _____ _____

_____ _____ _____ _____ _____

_____ _____ _____ _____ _____

_____ _____ _____ _____ _____

_____ _____ _____ _____ _____

3. The size of our drop-out rate for the past year: _____
   (Divide last year's total into total membership.)
   Ten-year average: _____

4. The average drop-out rate for our size church:
                                                 _____

   New/Suburbia = 2-3%   300+ members = 5-8%
   Stable/County = 3-5%   Old/Large = up to 15%

5. Over the past ten years, the average loss of membership by
   percentage:

   By Death   _____   National Average: 1-½%
   By Transfer   _____   2-3%
   By Withdrawal   _____   2-5%

   (total deaths divided by total membership; total transfers
   divided by total membership; total withdrawals divided by
   total membership)

6. Do we concentrate on assimilating new
   members within the first three months?   _____
7. Is a staff person, or a volunteer, responsible
   for assimilation of new members?   _____

8. Does our church have enough small groups
   for our size church?   _____
   To determine this number:
   a. divide worship attendance by 10:   _____
   b. count the number of small groups with
      less than 40 in attendance (include Sun-
      day school):   _____
   c. subtract (a) from (b) to determine the
      number over or under what is needed: _____

9. How many inactive families do we have?   _____

10. What percent of the congregation?   _____

11. Do we have a program to reinstate inactive
    members?   _____

12. Have we "cleaned our rolls" within the last
    3 years?   _____

13. Conclusion: _____

    _____

    _____

_____

Growth Principle Five: Growth Provides a Wider Outreach
                     to People in Need.

_____

1. List the total amounts of money given to all causes outside our
   congregation during the past ten years (most recent year first):

   _____   _____   _____

   _____   _____   _____

   _____   _____   _____

                                          _____

2. Does this increase or decrease correspond to the increase or
   the decrease in our average worship attendance?
                                                   _____

3. Conclusion: _____

_____

_____

_____

Growth Principle Six: Growth Need Not Be Hampered by
Participation in the Public Arena.

_____

1. List our programs that are social or political in nature:

_____

_____

_____

_____

_____

2. Do any of these programs attack the root
   causes of social injustice?   _____
3. How free is the pastor to preach or be involved in moral
   issues that are also political in nature?*   _____
4. Does our church understand that taking strong social stands
   will not harm the growth of the church?*   _____

5. Conclusion: _____

_____

_____

Worship Is the Number-one Building Block of Congregational Life

Growth Principle Seven: Growth Will Occur When Worship Is Intentionally Emphasized.

1. Do we consider worship the most important aspect of our ministry?* _____
2. Do we measure the size of our church by the number of people in worship, or by the actual membership?* _____
3. How many Sundays a year is there a sermon from our senior pastor? _____
4. How many Sundays a year does the service contain a sermon? _____
5. How many Sundays a year is there a sermon from our associate pastor? _____
6. Do the sermons speak to our personal needs?* _____
7. Does our pastor repeat sermons for no apparent reason?* _____
8. Do the Scriptures form the basis of the sermons?* _____
9. Do the sermons stimulate thought?* _____
10. Is our worship music pleasing to a majority of the congregation?* _____
11. Average size of present adult and youth choir(s) and hours they sing:

Hour	Size	No. Needed
_____	_____	_____
_____	_____	_____
_____	_____	_____

(To determine the proper size choir for each service, divide the attendance at each service by 10.)
12. Do we print out all elements of worship, such as the Gloria Patri, Doxology, etc.? _____

13. Is there a regular place in our bulletin designated for visitors?   _____

14. Is our bulletin the best piece of printed material we produce each week?*   _____

15. When we plan worship, do we consider the needs of visitors?   _____

16. Does every service offer an invitation to join?   _____

17. Does every service leave adequate opportunity for people to join the church?   _____

18. What is the ratio of worship attendance to membership?   _____

19. Do we have an attendance tracking system?   _____

20. Analysis of worship growth pattern for last 20 years (most recent year first).:

_____ _____%   _____ _____%

_____ _____%   _____ _____%

_____ _____%   _____ _____%

_____ _____%   _____ _____%

_____ _____%   _____ _____%

_____ _____%   _____ _____%

_____ _____%   _____ _____%

_____ _____%   _____ _____%

_____ _____%   _____ _____%

_____ _____%   _____ _____%

(Determine the percentage of growth between the years—difference between years 1 and 2 divided by year 1.)

Worship has increased/decreased _____% in the last 10 years.

Worship has increased/decreased _____% in the last 20 years.

21. Do we regularly keep track of worship patterns? _____

22. Do we respond to these patterns in any systematic fashion? _____

23. Money budgeted for worship: _____

    Is this 25% of the program budget? _____

24. Do we consider worship a form of drama?* _____

25. Do we plan, coordinate, and promote worship well in advance? _____

26. Do we regularly emphasize attendance at worship? _____

27. Do the ushers serve effectively as a team with the pastor(s)?* _____

28. Is there enough space for fellowship?* _____

29. Conclusion: _____

    _____

    _____

    _____

Growth Principle Eight: Growth Usually Occurs with the Addition of Each New Morning Worship Service.

1. How many services of morning worship? _____

   What are the hours? _____ _____ _____

2. Average attendance at each: _____ _____ _____

3. When was the newest service started? _____

4. Are we willing to provide an additional service of worship, even though our space may be adequate without it?* _____

5. Does each service have a regular choir? _____

6. Is there a youth choir that sings regularly? _____

7. Do we provide quality music at each service? _____

8. How many Sundays a year does our major adult choir sing? _____

9. How many musicals does it present each year? _____

10. Does our major adult choir take a vacation? _____

11. How many children's choirs? _____

How often do they sing? _____

12. Conclusion: _____

_____

_____

God Wants the Church to Grow

Growth Principle Nine: Growth Is Directly Related to the Leadership Strength of the Pastor.

1. Does our church understand that growth is directly related to the leadership of the pastor?* _____

2. Does our pastor assume leadership for the ministry of our church?* _____

3. Average tenure of all pastors the last 20 years: _____

4. Tenure of present pastor: _____

5. Are we willing to have a pastor stay at least 10 years?* _____

6. Are we willing to provide the kind of time away that is required by a long pastorate?* _____

7. How much vacation do our pastor(s) and/or staff receive?

_____

8. Does our pastor hold up a vision large enough to cause us to grow individually?* _____

9. Is our pastor a leader, rather than an enabler?* _____

10. Does our pastor cause things to happen in our church that would not happen otherwise?* _____

11. Does our pastor pull us into areas of ministry that we might not enter on our own?* _____

12. Does our pastor learn from mistakes?* _____

13. Does our pastor know how to delegate
    authority?   _____

    Does he or she do so?*   _____

14. Does our pastor consult us regularly about
    his/her vision for our church?*   _____

15. Has our pastor shown the ability to grow and develop new
    skills along with the growth of the church?*   _____

16. Is our pastor concerned with giving us what
    we need, rather than what we want?*   _____

17. Does our pastor possess the skills needed
    for our size church?   _____

18. Can our pastor respond and relate to a wide
    variety of religious expressions?*   _____

19. Is our pastor able to mediate between the
    various factions of the church?*   _____

20. Does our church have any concrete way to evaluate when it is
    time for the pastor to move?*   _____

21. Conclusion: _____

    _____

    _____

Growth Principle Ten: Growth Is Directly Related to the
Attitude of the Paid Staff.

1. Is the main responsibility of our paid staff to
   identify, recruit, train, lead, and deploy the
   laity into mission?   _____

2. Number of present staff: Program: _____

                               Support: _____

   Do we have one program staff member for
   every 100 in worship, or for every 300
   members, whichever is greater?   _____

3. Has the staff kept pace with growth?   _____

4. Are we staffed for *decline, maintenance,* or
   growth, based on answer to #2?   _____

5. What is the role of our associate pastor—
   apprentice; professional; retired?   _____

6. Is our support aimed at ministry rather than
   at record keeping?   _____

7. Does our pastor make use of the valuable
   information our paid staff knows about the
   congregation?*   _____

8. Is the relationship between our pastor and
   paid staff that of a team?*   _____

9. Does our paid staff have opportunities to
   develop both relational and functional
   skills?*   _____

10. Does our paid staff hold weekly meetings?*   _____

11. Does each paid staff member have an
    opportunity for input into the agenda?*   _____

12. Are new ideas from the paid staff welcome
    at meetings?*   _____

13. Does the paid staff have yearly retreats?   _____

14. Does the paid staff make sure all bases are
    covered on Sunday mornings?   _____

15. Do we hire some talented lay people instead
    of clergy?   _____

16. Does our paid staff require minimum
    supervision?   _____

17. Do we terminate paid staff members when
    we realize they are not able to do the job?   _____

18. Are we willing to pay higher salaries and be
    content with fewer paid staff?   _____

19. Adequate total salaries:
    0-200 in worship = 60% of total budget
    200+ in worship = 40% of total budget
    What percent of our budget do our salaries
    represent?   _____

    Are our total salaries adequate?   _____

20. Does our paid staff consist mainly of
    specialists?   _____

21. Do we negotiate paid staff positions for
    longer than one year?   _____

22. Do we evaluate new paid staff members
    after three months?   _____

23. Do we have measurable job descriptions for each staff member which clearly list the objectives to be achieved during the year? _____

24. Is there a certain time each week set aside by the pastor when individual paid staff members can make appointments? _____

25. Does the pastor share his/her vision for the congregation at staff meetings? _____

26. Has our staff had formal training in time management? _____

27. Conclusion: _____

_____

_____

_____

Growth Principle Eleven: Growth Is Directly Related to the Unpaid Staff's Perception of the Congregation's Size and Ability, Rather Than the Reality.

1. Use the following chart to determine the actual size of our church in relation to other United Methodist churches:

Average Worship Attendance	% of UM Churches
0-49	40.5%
50-74	57.5%
75-99	69.1%
100-149	81.6%
150-199	88.6%
200-349	96.3%
350-499	98.4%
500-749	99.3%
750-999	99.6%
1000+	99.7%

Based on these figures, our church is larger than _____% of all United Methodist churches.

These figures are for United Methodist churches, but are within a very few percentage points for all mainline Protestant denominations. Adapted from: Department of Statistics, General Council on Finance and Administration, The United Methodist Church.

2. How would we describe our church in relation to other churches —Small, Medium, Large, Very Large?*   _____

3. Is our lay leadership's perception of our church's size the same as the reality? Compare #2 to #1.   _____

4. Does our lay leadership communicate to the congregation a realistic perception of our church's size and ability?*   _____

5. Does our congregation have a realistic perception of our church's size and ability?   _____

6. Does our lay leadership carry out the official vision of the church in ways that meet the needs of the congregation?*   _____

7. Is our lay leadership objective concerning major issues and decisions?*   _____

8. Does our lay leadership know the difference between opinion and judgment?*   _____

9. Can our lay leadership suspend judgment long enough to make intelligent decisions?*   _____

10. Can our lay leadership accept and appreciate people with different viewpoints?*   _____

11. Are at least half of our lay leaders new to the institutional church?*   _____

12. Is our lay leadership accessible to the rest of the congregation?*   _____

13. Does our lay leadership have the necessary time and energy?*   _____

14. Does our lay leadership cause things to happen?*   _____

15. Does each of our lay leaders have a large following in the congregation?*   _____

16. Is the tenure of our lay leaders limited to three years?*   _____

17. Does new lay leadership surface on a regular basis?*   _____

18. How many leaders do we have?   _____
    (Definition of a leader: has a following and will use that
    following to cause things to happen.)
19. Do we have one leadership position for
    every 15 members of the church?   _____
20. What is our greatest challenge in developing lay leaders
    —recruitment, training, identification,
    deployment?   _____

God Expects the Best We Have to Offer

Growth Principle Twelve: When 80 Percent of any Space Is in Use, It Is Time to Make Plans for More.

1. What level of commitment do we expect from
   our members—high, medium, low?   _____
2. In the past, has our church missed any
   windows of opportunity?   _____
3. Does our church understand that we can use
   only 80% of our space?*   _____
4. What is the total and individual square feet of
   all our facilities, excluding the sanctuary? _____
   (Measure each class separately, as well as sanctuary and
   nursery. Keep records of the square feet of each to answer #10.)
   a. Total Sunday school space   _____

   b. Fellowship hall   _____

   c. Other   _____

5. Do we need more worship space?   _____
   (Do not estimate or take an architect's word. Have several
   people sit down on a pew and measure what is comfortable,
   then compute throughout the sanctuary. Or measure actual
   pew lengths and divide by 22 inches.)
   a. Sanctuary capacity: _____
   b. 80% of capacity: _____
   c. Average main attendance: _____
      (If (c) is larger than (b), the answer to #5 is yes.)

6. Is worship capacity more than 50% larger
   than Sunday school capacity?   _____
   (To get answer, double #5b and compare with #9b.)

7. Do we need more choir space?   _____

   a. Choir capacity: _____

   b. 80% of capacity: _____

   c. Average main attendance: _____
      (If (c) is larger than (b), the answer to #7 is yes.)

8. Do we need more nursery space?   _____

   a. Nursery capacity?   _____

   b. 80% of capacity: _____

   c. Average main attendance: _____
      (If (c) is larger than (b), the answer to #8 is yes.)

   How many personnel at main attendance?   _____
   Is there a nursery for all events?   _____

   Are infants and toddlers separated?   _____
   Are any nursery policies given to the
   mothers?   _____

9. Do we need more education space?   _____

   a. Education capacity from #4a: _____

   b. 80% of capacity: _____

   c. Average main attendance: _____
      (If (c) is larger than (b), the answer to #9 is yes.)

10. Is each Sunday school class under 80%?   _____
    (Allow 30 square feet per person for kindergarten and under;
    20 square feet per person for first grade and up. Draw a floor
    plan for each level of each building and show the capacity of
    each room and the average attendance of the class.)

11. Which classes are over 80% or near it?

    _____

    Do we need to rearrange any of these classes?

    _____

    _____

12. Number of classrooms available: _____

Number of classrooms presently used: _____

13. Sunday school average attendance for last 20 years, including percentage over previous year:

_____ _____%   _____ _____%

_____ _____%   _____ _____%

_____ _____%   _____ _____%

_____ _____%   _____ _____%

_____ _____%   _____ _____%

_____ _____%   _____ _____%

_____ _____%   _____ _____%

_____ _____%   _____ _____%

_____ _____%   _____ _____%

_____ _____%   _____ _____%

Sunday School attendance has increased/decreased _____% over the past ten years.

14. Do we have more than one session of Sunday school?   _____

    Attendance at each: _____ _____

15. According to the 80% rule, does our church need to add space?   _____

    If so, where?   _____

16. Conclusion: _____

    _____

    _____

    _____

Growth Principle Thirteen: Growth Is Encouraged When Parking Is Adequate.

1. Does our church own enough land? If less than 8 acres, is there adjacent property for sale?
   We own: _____
   We need: _____
2. Does our congregation understand the radical changes in parking needs during the last twenty years?* _____
3. Average attendance of largest service: _____
   (If Sunday school and worship occur at the same hour, count the total number at that hour.)
4. Average number of people per car: _____
5. Paved off-street parking spaces available: _____
   (please count)
6. 80% of the total parking spaces: _____
7. Number of spaces needed to accommodate attendance: (divide #4 into #3) _____
8. How many spaces do we need to add? _____
   (If #7 is larger than #6, more spaces are needed. If #6 is larger than #7, no more spaces are needed. Remember—this is an immediate need and does not consider future growth. [Note: March 1987 survey reported 2.66 people per household. This compares to 2.76 in 1980 and 3.58 in 1970. Source: Bureau of the Census, P-20, No. 417])
9. Do people have trouble finding a parking space on Sunday morning?* _____
   If so, at what hour do they arrive? _____
10. Conclusion: _____
   _____
   _____

Growth Principle Fourteen: Growth Can Occur Even Though a Church Cannot Afford to Build.

1. How much is the approximate yearly debt service on the new facility we need? _____
2. Our total indebtedness is: _____
   (see Growth Principle Seventeen, #29)

3. The ratio of our present debt service to our
   budget is: _____
   (See Growth Principle Seventeen, #29. It should not exceed
   30% of total budget.)
4. The ratio of our debt service to budget, with
   new facility added, will be: _____
   (Add #1 to #3. Amount should not exceed 33% of the total.)
5. When was the last building program?   _____
6. What was built? _____
7. Conclusion: _____

   _____

   _____

Growth Principle Fifteen: Growth Can Occur Without Merely Transferring Members from One Church to Another.

1. Breakdown of new members for the past ten years (most recent
   year first):

Prof. of Faith	Other Denom.	UM Transfer		Total
_____	_____	_____	=	___
_____	_____	_____	=	___
_____	_____	_____	=	___
_____	_____	_____	=	___
_____	_____	_____	=	___
_____	_____	_____	=	___
_____	_____	_____	=	___
_____	_____	_____	=	___
_____	_____	_____	=	___
_____	_____	_____	=	___

2. Do we practice spiritual inbreeding, concentrating mainly on confirmands, infant
   baptisms, and transfers?   _____

3. Does column 1 outnumber columns 2 and 3?   _____

4. Do we intentionally reach out to non-
   Methodists?   _____

5. What is the average number of *miles* our
   members drive to work?   _____
   (Answers to #5–7 are taken from the four-week survey in
   worship.)

6. What is the average number of *minutes* our
   members drive to work?   _____

7. What is the average number of *miles* our
   members drive to church?   _____
   (If #5 is larger than #7, concentrate on meeting the needs of
   the people represented in those miles.)

8. How many people live in this radius?   _____
   Remember that 60% of these are unchurched prospects.
   (Answers to #8–13 can be obtained through the Chamber of
   Commerce.)

9. Who are these unchurched people?

   Singles never married   _____

   Single-parent families   _____

   Singles divorced   _____

   Young families   _____

   Older families   _____

   Senior citizens   _____

   Upper/Middle/Lower class   _____

   Black/White/Brown/Yellow   _____

10. Which groups are not being adequately ministered to in our
    area? (Call the churches in your area and inquire what
    programs they offer.)

    _____

    _____

11. Has the population of our county increased or decreased over
    the last 10 years?   _____
    By how much?   _____

12. Has our church kept pace with the popula-
    tion increase/decrease?   _____

13. Are the schools full in our area?   _____
    (If the schools are full and growing, there is great potential for
    growth.)

14. Conclusion: _____

    _____

    _____

Growth Principle Sixteen: Growth Almost Always Occurs If the Congregation Is Friendly Toward Visitors.

1. How does our church feel about the parables of the one lost
   sheep (Matt. 18:10-14), the new wine (Matt. 9:16-17), the great
   commission (Matt. 28:18-20), Jesus' commission to the disciples
   in the upper room (Acts 1:6-8), the difference between Paul and
   the church at Jerusalem (Acts 15), and the loaves and the fishes
   (John 6:1-14)?*

   _____

   _____

   _____

   _____

2. How many dollars and what percent of our budget goes to the
   following forms of advertising?

   Yellow Pages $_____ _____ %

   Newspaper   _____ _____

   Flyers   _____ _____

   Radio   _____ _____

   Television   _____ _____

   Direct Mail   _____ _____

   Other   _____ _____

   TOTAL $_____ _____ %

Does the total amount represent 5% of our
budget?   _____

3. How many new families visit each week?   _____

Do we contact them within 48 hours?   _____

4. What percent of these families join?   _____
(Multiply #3 by 52 and divide that number into the number of
new families for the year.)

5. What brought these families to our church?
Friends and relatives   _____

Driving by   _____

Newspaper   _____

Yellow Pages   _____

Preschool   _____

Singles   _____

Television   _____

Banner   _____

Direct Mail   _____

Other   _____
(Note: It is not uncommon for 25 to 35% of first-time visitors to
attend because of advertising [other than by friends and
relatives].)

6. How many contacts are made each week
with unchurched people?   _____

7. Does someone on our staff spend twenty
hours each week visiting the unchurched?   _____

8. Do we make it clear in worship that we
expect visitors each Sunday?   _____

Does our bulletin reflect this?   _____

9. Do we use every event in the life of our
church as an entry point for membership?   _____

10. How many visitors are on our mailing list
each week?   _____

11. Do we put visitors on the mailing list the
first time they visit?   _____

12. Do we promote Christmas Eve services
through adequate space and advertising?   _____

13. Do our paid and unpaid staff know the importance of Christmas Eve and respond accordingly—choir, sermons, ushers, etc.?* _____

14. Do we have adequate exterior and interior signs around the church?* _____

15. Do we have an adequate number of trained greeters?* _____

16. Do we provide separate registration cards for visitors? _____

17. Do we have an evangelism team? _____

18. What group of people or segment of the population can we reach that no one else is ministering to? (See Growth Principle Fifteen #10) _____

19. Do we designate 10 percent of our parking spaces for visitors? _____

20. Do our members wear name tags? _____

21. Does our church have a New Members class? _____

22. Do we provide tours of the facilities? _____

23. When at church, do the members go out of their way to meet and welcome people they don't know?* _____

24. Do the members pray regularly that the church will grow spiritually and numerically?* _____

25. Do we provide information packets for visitors? _____

26. Is the appearance of our property pleasing?* _____

27. Do we have an information booth or designated area for information? _____

If so, is it well marked? _____

28. Conclusion: _____

_____

_____

_____

Growth Principle Seventeen: Asking for Money
Encourages Growth.

1. Budget totals for the past ten years, including operational and debt service (this is not income):

   _____   _____

   _____   _____

   _____   _____

   _____   _____

   _____   _____

2. Does our church often talk about money and financial stewardship?*   _____

3. Do we avoid telling people the church needs their money and talk instead about people's need to become stewards?*   _____

4. Does the preparation of our pledge drives involve at least ¼ of our worshiping congregation?   _____

5. Does our leadership understand the importance of pledge Sunday?*   _____

6. Do we have a pledge drive every year for the budget?   _____

7. What time of the year is the pledge drive?   _____

8. Do we have at least three weeks of education prior to pledging?   _____

9. Does our pledge card ask only for money?   _____

10. What role does the pastor play in the pledge drive?*

    _____

11. Number of pledges and averages for the past five years:

NO. OF PLDGS.	AVG. AMT.	TOTAL PLDGD.	BUDGET	% OF BUDGET
_____ x	_____ =	_____	_____	_____
_____ x	_____ =	_____	_____	_____
_____ x	_____ =	_____	_____	_____
_____ x	_____ =	_____	_____	_____
_____ x	_____ =	_____	_____	_____

12. Do our pledges underwrite more than 70 to
    90% of our budget?   _____

13. Have pledges increased or decreased?   _____

14. Based on our record, what kind of income can we expect next
    year, if we do nothing different?
    Pledges from new members $_____
    Loose plate   _____
    Regular nonpledger   _____
    Building-usage fees   _____
    Foundation   _____
    Special offerings   _____
    Sunday school offerings   _____
    Interest   _____
    Memorials   _____
    Other   _____
    TOTAL $_____

    (If you discount your total pledges to reflect your historical
    pledge loss, then count your anticipated pledges from new
    members after you have divided them by ½. If you do not
    discount the total pledges, then do not count anticipated
    new-member pledges.)

15. Do we select our stewardship leaders on the basis of their
    giving patterns and willingness to give of
    themselves?   _____

16. Do we contact new members for a pledge? _____

17. Do we keep records of giving and pledge
    patterns and analyze them regularly?   _____

18. Is our pledge program centered around
    tithing?   _____

19. How are campaigns conducted? _____

    _____

20. Analysis of last three stewardship programs: ——————

——

——

21. Do we encourage designated giving and discourage a unified budget?   ——————

22. Does our pledge card offer us choices?   ——————

23. Does our Christmas offering equal at least half of one month's additional income?   ——————

24. Do we personalize our pledge program?   ——————

25. Do we have regular special offerings for items within the budget?   ——————

26.

Worship Average Last 10 Yrs.	Ratio of Budget to Worship	Ratio of Bgtd. Income to Worship
————	————	————
————	————	————
————	————	————
————	————	————
————	————	————
————	————	————
————	————	————
————	————	————
————	————	————
————	————	————

(To compute ratio of budget to worship, divide worship total into budget total for each year. To compute ratio of budget income to worship, divide worship total into budgeted income total for each year.)

27. Does our total budget income (operating and building) equal or exceed $1,000 for every person in worship on an average Sunday? (See above list.)   ——————

28. Does ⅓ of our church's income come from more than ¼ of our pledges?   ——————

29.

Total Indebtedness Last 10 Yrs.	Ratio of Indebtedness to Budget	Budgeted Debt Service Last 10 Yrs.	Ratio of Debt Service to Budget
_____	_____	_____	_____
_____	_____	_____	_____
_____	_____	_____	_____
_____	_____	_____	_____
_____	_____	_____	_____
_____	_____	_____	_____
_____	_____	_____	_____
_____	_____	_____	_____

(To compute ratio of indebtedness to budget, divide budget total into indebtedness totals for each year. To compute ratio of debt service to budget, divide budget total into budgeted debt service total for each year.)

30. Is our debt service under 30% of our total operating and building budget? (See above list.) _____

31.

Budgeted Income* Last 10 Yrs.	Ratio of Debt Service to Bgtd. Income	Ratio of Indebtedness to Bgtd. Income
_____	_____	_____
_____	_____	_____
_____	_____	_____
_____	_____	_____
_____	_____	_____
_____	_____	_____
_____	_____	_____
_____	_____	_____

(*Budgeted income is the actual amount of money raised each year that can be used against the budget. Therefore the figures in #1 and #31 should *not* be the same. To compute ratio of debt service to budgeted income, divide budgeted income into budgeted debt service totals for each year. To compute ratio of indebtedness to budgeted income, divide budgeted income into total indebtedness totals for each year.)

32. Analysis of growth over last 10 years:

Budget Growth   _____

Total Indebtedness Growth   _____

Debt Service Growth   _____

Budgeted Income Growth   _____

Worship Growth   _____

(Take current year minus first-year totals; divide that number by the first year.)

33. Breakdown of Current Budget:

	19_____	Target	Over/Under
Salaries	_____	40%	_____
Debt	_____	25%	_____
Program	_____	10%	_____
Outreach	_____	15%	_____
Advertising	_____	5%	_____
Stewardship	_____	1%	_____

(Note: The above targets leave only 4% for maintenance, office, etc. For many churches this is impossible. This analysis does point up the difficulty growing churches have and the need to keep debt service under 30%. Churches that wish to give a higher percentage to outreach will need to use a different formula and structure the budget differently.)

34. How much of our budget is in other categories?   _____

35. List of Financial Resources:

    Endowments   _____

    Wills   _____

    Capital Fund Pledges   _____

    Cash Reserves   _____

    Foundation   _____

    Stocks and Bonds   _____

    Other   _____

    TOTAL   _____

36. Is there a plan to use this money?   _____

    (It discourages good stewardship practices for congregations to have large sums of ready money to rely on for everyday expenses.)

37. Before we retire a mortgage, do we designate a new ministry to use that same amount of money?   _____

38. Do we allow the use of plaques?   _____

39. Do we avoid cutting the budget at all costs?*   _____

40. Do we look for new ways to raise money each year?*   _____

41. When was the last capital fund drive?   _____

42. Does our pastor know what each member gives?   _____

43. Conclusion: _____

_____

_____

_____

Growth Principle Eighteen: Long-term Growth Needs a Solid Foundation.

1. Does our church have an overall vision for
   its ministry and future?*   _____
2. Does our church have a mission statement
   that is clear, concise, and openended?   _____
3. Does our church have a logo?   _____
4. Does our church have an anthem?   _____
5. If so, are these used consistently?   _____
6. Do we have a regularly updated five- or
   ten-year plan?   _____
7. Do we have a master plan for the use of land
   and facilities?   _____
8. When was the last time we did strategic
   planning?   _____
9. What is our church's main strength?*   _____

10. What is our church's main weakness?*

    _____

    _____

    _____

Growth Principle Nineteen: Regular Strategic Planning
        Is Necessary for Healthy Growth.

    _____

1. Where does our church want to go?*
2. Does our church know *what* we must do *now*
   in order to arrive at that destination?*   _____
3. List present officially adopted objectives (goals) of the church:

    _____

    _____

    _____

4. What are our short-term objectives?*

    _____

    _____

    _____

5. What are our long-term objectives?*

_____

_____

_____

6. Are these objectives people-centered and measurable?* _____

7. Do the objectives of our pastor and the church match?* _____

8. Do we celebrate when we reach an objective?* _____

9. Do our objectives keep us from becoming more interested in numbers than in people?* _____

10. Do we have checklists for our objectives? Do we follow them?* _____

11. When we delegate, are we careful to select people whose skills match the tasks?* _____

12. Do we hold people accountable?* _____

13. When asking people to do a job, do we let them know we expect their best?* _____

14. Do our objectives have timelines?* _____

15. Do we evaluate each program or strategy? _____

16. Do we often spend too much time setting objectives and not enough time implementing them?* _____

17. Conclusion: _____

_____

_____

_____

Growth Principle Twenty: It Takes More Effort to Implement Change Than to Maintain the Status Quo or Exercise Veto Power.

1. Is our church free from power cliques?*   _____
3. Do one or two people derail things the
   majority want?*   _____
4. Does our church worry too much about
   hurting pepole's feelings and not enough
   about being in ministry?*   _____
5. Conclusion: _____

_____

A Pastor's Plan

The following Pastor's Plan is offered as a starting point after completion of the Ministry Audit.

1. Begin the Ministry Audit with a personal assessment of your own attitude toward the mission of the church. Do you have a clear vision of where you want this church to be in twenty years, and are you willing to take it there? Do you believe, and are you willing to act upon the premise that God wants your church to grow and be healthy? The smaller the church, the more important your attitude.

2. If your attitude is right, then no matter what size your church, take a good look at what happens in worship. Is the service relevant? Does the sermon speak to the everyday needs of the person in the pew? Are the music down to earth, easily understood, and lively? Are the space and environment comfortable? Does the bulletin welcome Joe? Do you offer a choice of worship hours?

3. Gather a small group of core leaders who share your vision for the church—people who are objective enough to see beyond their own personal needs. Begin to lead them to discover how they can make the common vision happen in ways that meet their needs.

4. Next, is there an off-street parking space for every two people on the church grounds at the peak hour? The larger the church and the less rural the area, the more important this ratio. What are your church's actual needs according to the Ministry Audit? Is there land to buy or ground to pave?

5. Make sure your program staff equals one person for every 100 people in worship. There is no point to bringing people in the front door if they go out the back door.

6. Identify a need in your area and fill it. People need a reason to drive to your church, if they can just as easily drive across town to a church that meets their needs.

7. If there is a solid mission, are you telling the area about it through advertising and word of mouth, and are you known for this mission throughout the area? Ask your secretary what most calls from the public are about.

8. Begin a solid stewardship program of percentage giving and tithing. From the start, let it be known that you personally are a tither and expect others to follow your lead. Don't be afraid to upset people when you talk about money. Remember, for many people, money is their false God.

9. How are you doing with the 80 percent factor? Do you need to provide additional space? Start with parking, please!

10. Do you add all first-time visitors to your mailing list? Are they contacted within twenty-four hours, and at least four times the first week?

11. From here, go with whatever needs the most strengthening and attention. May the grace of God go before you!

CHART 1

SURVEY FORM FOR WORSHIP

(Conduct in worship for four consecutive Sundays. Have each person fill one out each Sunday, even though one was filled out the previous week.)

1. My age is:

   _____ 18–20

   _____ 21–34

   _____ 35–50

   _____ 50+

2. My sex is:

   _____ Male

   _____ Female

3. My marital status is:

   _____ Married

   _____ Single

4. The number of people in my car this morning: _____

5. The number of miles I drive to **church**: _____

6. The number of miles I drive to **work**: _____

7. The number of *minutes* I drive to **work**: _____

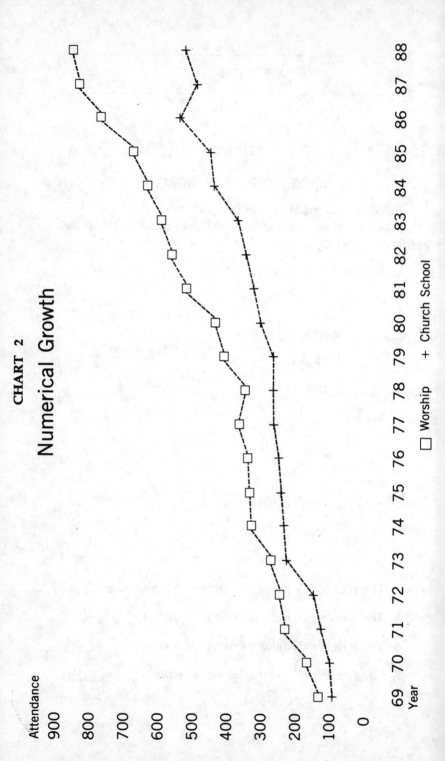

CHART 2
Numerical Growth

CHART 3

Relation of Staff to Growth

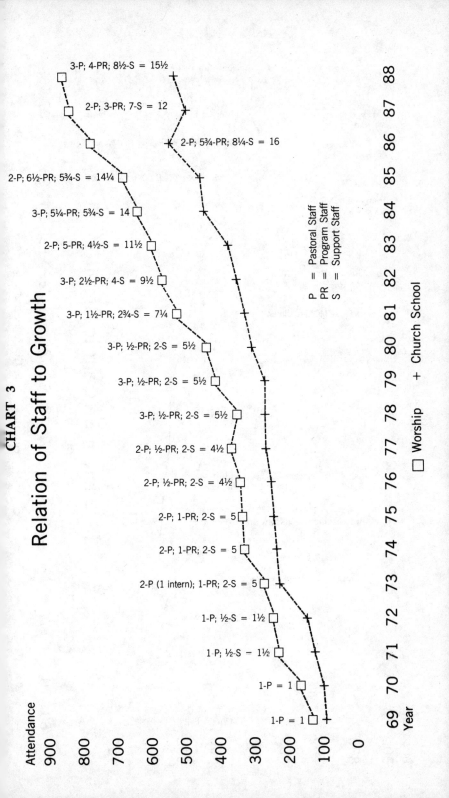

3-P; 4-PR; 8½-S = 15½

2-P; 3-PR; 7-S = 12

2-P; 5¾-PR; 8¼-S = 16

2-P; 6½-PR; 5¾-S = 14¼

3-P; 5¼-PR; 5¾-S = 14

2-P; 5-PR; 4½-S = 11½

3-P; 2½-PR; 4-S = 9½

3-P; 1½-PR; 2¾-S = 7¼

3-P; ½-PR; 2-S = 5½

3-P; ½-PR; 2-S = 5½

3-P; ½-PR; 2-S = 5½

2-P; ½-PR; 2-S = 4½

2-P; ½-PR; 2-S = 4½

2-P; 1-PR; 2-S = 5

2-P; 1-PR; 2-S = 5

2-P (1 intern); 1-PR; 2-S = 5

1-P; ½-S = 1½

1-P; ½-S = 1½

1-P = 1

1-P = 1

P = Pastoral Staff
PR = Program Staff
S = Support Staff

Attendance
900
800
700
600
500
400
300
200
100
0

Year
69 70 71 72 73 74 75 76 77 78 79 80 81 82 83 84 85 86 87 88

□ Worship   + Church School

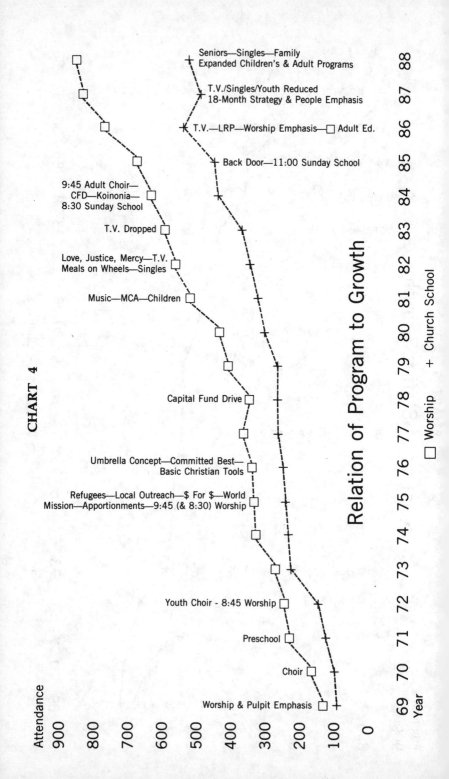

CHART 4

Relation of Program to Growth

Attendance

900 — 800 — 700 — 600 — 500 — 400 — 300 — 200 — 100 — 0

Year: 69 70 71 72 73 74 75 76 77 78 79 80 81 82 83 84 85 86 87 88

☐ Worship   + Church School

Seniors—Singles—Family
Expanded Children's & Adult Programs

T.V./Singles/Youth Reduced
18-Month Strategy & People Emphasis

T.V.—LRP—Worship Emphasis—☐ Adult Ed.

Back Door—11:00 Sunday School

9:45 Adult Choir—
CFD—Koinonia—
8:30 Sunday School

T.V. Dropped

Love, Justice, Mercy—T.V.
Meals on Wheels—Singles

Music—MCA—Children

Capital Fund Drive

Umbrella Concept—Committed Best—
Basic Christian Tools

Refugees—Local Outreach—$ For $—World
Mission—Apportionments—9:45 (& 8:30) Worship

Youth Choir - 8:45 Worship

Preschool

Choir

Worship & Pulpit Emphasis

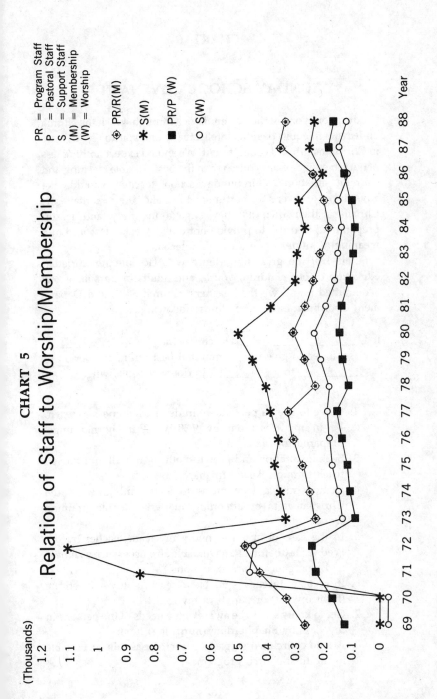

CHART 5

Relation of Staff to Worship/Membership

PR = Program Staff
P = Pastoral Staff
S = Support Staff
(M) = Membership
(W) = Worship

◈ PR/R(M)
∗ S(M)
■ PR/P (W)
○ S(W)

(Thousands)

1.2
1.1
1
0.9
0.8
0.7
0.6
0.5
0.4
0.3
0.2
0.1
0

69 70 71 72 73 74 75 76 77 78 79 80 81 82 83 84 85 86 87 88 Year

CHART 6

SUNDAY SCHOOL COVENANT

Education is one of the key ministries through which the church endeavors to equip persons intellectually and spiritually to share in Christian faith and commitment. We should expect nothing less of ourselves and of our church than the best possible teaching and learning situations. Our Sunday school teachers should take advantage of every opportunity to make their heritage as Christians their own as they engage in study and lesson preparation, in order to provide not only a weekly lesson, but a meaningful influence on those they teach.

Because of the great importance we place on the Christian education of our children, youth, and adults in pursuit of our "committed best," we the Teachers, Church Staff, and Department Coordinators do agree to the following:

I. I, _____, a teacher of the _____ class, agree to give my "committed best" from the period of _____ to _____ in doing the following:

1. Strive to keep a personal attitude of willingness to teach.
2. Be in my classroom by 9:30 A.M. Sunday mornings, prepared to teach.
3. Seek inspiration and growth both for myself and those I teach through Basic Christian Tools I.
4. Demonstrate a willingness to learn and grow in the Christian faith by attending quarterly planning/training workshops.
5. In the case of absence, notify my team teacher by the Wednesday before. (Unavoidable absences, such as illness and emergencies, are exceptions.)
6. If my team teacher is unable to teach, notify a substitute (from my list) or parent of my need.
7. Get to know and to be aware of the needs of the persons in my class by Shepherding (nurturing) them.
8. Attend church worship and participate as fully as possible in the total church program.

II. We, the Church Staff and the Department Coordinators, agree to give our "committed best" to support the Sunday school teachers by providing the following:

1. Whole-family participation in Christian education and encouragement of parents' involvement in their children's classes.
2. Curriculum, resources, and supplies.
3. Teacher orientation and training.
4. Quarterly planning/training workshops.
5. Continual evaluation of current Christian education programs and the seeking and support of new ideas.
6. Special materials and support of creative and/or innovative efforts which further the objective of Christian education.
7. Provide a clean, well-lit, furnished room.

Agreed to and approved this _____ day of _____,
19____

_____   _____
TEACHER   DIRECTOR

_____   _____
DEPT. COORDINATOR   PASTOR

_____   _____
DEPT. COORDINATOR   PASTOR

CHART 7

LEADER COMMITTED BEST

As a leader of Colonial Hills United Methodist Church in 1988, I covenant with the church to give my COMMITTED BEST to my position of leadership. I will strive faithfully to fulfill all the responsibilities of my position. I will work in cooperation with the staff and lay leadership to build up the Body of Christ. I understand that I can depend on the church for needed support, resources, and training.

_____   _____
          Leader   Pastor or Staff Person

_____
          Date

CHART 8

MEMBER COMMITTED BEST

As a disciple of Jesus Christ and a member of Colonial Hills United Methodist Church, I covenant to give my "Committed Best" to my Lord and my church during 1988. Specifically, I covenant:

to reflect the spirit and ethic of Christ in my relationships;

to grow in my knowledge of God through reading and study of Scripture;

to seek opportunities to translate my faith into action;

to support my church with prayers, presence, gifts, and service.

Signature _____ Date _____

(Please place on altar table as you come forward for communion.)

CHART 9

PARENT "COMMITTED BEST" COVENANT

Deut. 6:4-7 is a statement of faith followed by the challenge to educate: Hear, O Israel the Lord our God is one Lord; and you shall love the Lord your God with all your heart, and with all your soul, and with all your might. And these words which I command you this day shall be upon your heart; and you shall teach them diligently to your children, and shall talk of them when you sit in your house, and when you walk by the way, and when you lie down and when you rise.

The parents of _____ agree to give our "Committed Best" in the nurturing process of our child. We acknowledge both the privilege and the responsibility of insuring a quality Christian education for our young person. We therefore covenant to:

* communicate the seriousness of regular church school attendance
* have our child/youth present on time
* pick our child/youth up on time
* review and discuss material he/she brings home
* participate in child's classroom (visit, help with projects, parties, learning centers)
* encourage stewardship education
* provide my child with a Bible and encourage him/her to bring it to church
* get to know my child's teachers

Agreed and approved this _____ day of _____ , 19__

_____
Parent(s) Signature

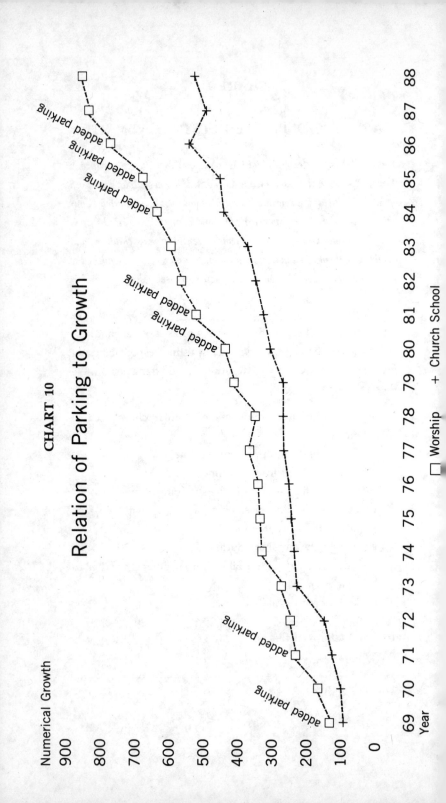

CHART 10

Relation of Parking to Growth

Numerical Growth

900
800
700
600
500
400
300
200
100
0

added parking
added parking
added parking
added parking
added parking
added parking
added parking

69 70 71 72 73 74 75 76 77 78 79 80 81 82 83 84 85 86 87 88
Year

□ Worship   + Church School

CHART 11

VISITORS' CORNER

Welcome to Colonial Hills UMC, better known as the Umbrella Church. The Umbrella is our symbol because of the diversity of our ministry and because our membership is open to all people committed to Christ. Stressing this symbol, we have become a diverse yet united fellowship.

I Corinthians 12:4-26 tells us that "there are a variety of gifts, but the same spirit." John Wesley put it this way: "In the essentials—unity; in the non-essentials—freedom; in all things— love." Rather than seeking conformity, we grow upon the richness of our diversity.

Our Mission Statement: "We are the people of God, called to live under the Umbrella of Love, Justice, and Mercy, to nurture the churched and win the unchurched."

An Umbrella Church is an exciting arena to serve Christ. Come join us!

TO JOIN OUR CHURCH TODAY
(Present this to pastor during final hymn)

Name(s) _____ Phone _____

Address_____

Children—Birthdays _____

You may join by:

Profession of faith _____ Restoration of Vows _____
Transfer of membership _____
Baptism & Profession of Faith _____
Children/Youth joining
  as full members _____ Preparatory Roll _____
Former Church _____
Address _____

CHART 12

PLEDGE CARD

COLONIAL HILLS UNITED METHODIST CHURCH

Yes, I (we) will step up to tithing by (please check one):

_____ Pledging 10% or more of my (our) annual income (gross or net) to God

_____ Pledging to increase my (our) pledge to God by 1% of my (our) annual income (gross or net)

_____ Pledging to increase my (our) financial pledge to God

_____ Pledging to God for the first time

Please use my (our) gift as follows: *I pledge my (our) gift:*
                                                 (check one)

$_____ for General Budget   _____ Weekly

$_____ for Building Debt
        Retirement   _____ Monthly

$_____ for Apportionments   _____ Quarterly

$_____ for Outreach Ministries
(specify)   _____ Yearly

                                     _____ Other

$_____ TOTAL FOR FISCAL 19_____

NAME: _____

ADDRESS & ZIP: _____

SIGNATURE: _____

I (we) understand that this commitment begins April 1, 19_____ and concludes March 31, 19_____ and may be revised at any time by notifying the Church Administrator.

CHART 13

18-MONTH STRATEGY

I. Goal: To have a healthy people-centered ministry and a balanced budget in 18 months.

II. Biblical Basis: "All things work together for the good of those that love the Lord." We are going to shift from a program-centered ministry to a people-centered ministry. Something very good is going to come from this present financial crisis.

III. Basic strategy has dual emphasis: 1/2 of our energy and money will be spent on nurturing our present congregation, and 1/2 of our energy and money will be spent on evangelism.

IV. Action Plan: To reach this goal in 18 months the following action is suggested:

    A. Job descriptions of staff will be changed from program to people orientation at the direction of the Senior Pastor.

    B. Pastoral staff must spend the majority of its time one-on-one with the members.

    C. To accomplish the above, the pastors must be freed from all meetings such as COM, Finance, and Executive Committee.

    D. Committees will be handled the following way:

        1. Have fewer committee meetings.

        2. Administrative board will meet monthly.

        3. Executive committee will meet with Senior Pastor to make all financial decisions for the next twelve months. Senior Pastor will make recommendations to the committee.

        4. All committee members are asked to volunteer to open their homes up once or twice during the next twelve months for parties with members, visitors, and their friends to meet the pastors. All that would be provided is a light dessert. There will be two of these a week.

E. There are several ways to restructure the staff. The goal is to reduce present staff by $30,000. Present staff will be interviewed to see who can fit where and who wishes to remain under the new guidelines. Rationale: We will either do this now and be solvent in 18 months, or we will gradually lose staff over the next few months and be in an even worse situation 12 months from now.

F. We will move from program-oriented staff to people-oriented staff. Instead of spending money to create programs, we will provide people opportunities in homes and around the church that encourage fellowship without spending church money. Retreats will be encouraged with the members paying the entire cost.

G. From now on, no staff will be hired unless we can pay salaries that are competitive with other churches. We also must begin rewarding those staff who remain with us and reach the goals set by bringing their salaries up to par with persons in comparable positions in other churches before hiring other staff.

H. Discontinue positions of bookkeeper and one secretary. Provide a secretarial pool for one year.

I. Prioritize secretarial time to those activities which directly involve evangelism, new member assimilation, coordination of volunteers, and all church visitation. No program staff will need to do secretarial work.

J. The position of Director of Adult Ministries will be discontinued. The pastors will pick up the responsibilities.

K. In order to retain the Children's Director and Youth Director full time there must be a fund raiser in the amount of $9,000.

L. Do whatever is necessary to build chancel choir to 45 average attendance. This is a key factor in raising the satisfaction level of the congregation and attracting new members. Present choir leaders have agreed to try to do this on their own. If there is not a marked increase within two months, they have agreed to obtain four sectional assistants for recruiting, sectional rehearsals, and singing in choir.

M. Improve the joining rate of first-time visitors so that 20-30% join within three to six months.

N. The Senior Pastor, along with the Executive Committee, will decide how to allocate what money is available. The allocation of money will be prioritized around the needs of worship and evangelism. Program expense would be decided upon by Senior Pastor and Executive Committee.

O. The T.V. ministry will continue as reruns for the remainder of the year. The cost will be either $2,500 or $5,000, the Executive Committee to decide.

P. Senior Pastor will make a commitment to the above program, no matter what appointment he is offered in the next 18 months. After we are successful, the T.V. ministry will be the first outreach program reinstated after apportionments and before adding any more staff.

Q. If there is any balance of money at the end of the year, it will go to Apportionments.

The above proposal has the unanimous endorsement of both the Pastor Parish Committee and the Finance Committee.

CHART 14

COLONIAL HILLS
FUTURES COMMITTEE REPORT

November 1988

The Committee's History

In mid-1988, the Futures Committee was authorized by the Administrative Board to examine the future needs of Colonial Hills and to report the findings to the December 1988 Charge Conference. The intent of this report was to give a brief preview of an extended report to be voted up or down by the Leadership Conference in January 1989.

Between October and December the Futures Committee met six times. The eight-member committee examined and discussed the past, present, and future status of resources, including staff, space, and money.

This report acknowledges the successful completion of the 18-Month Plan and believes that with the Stewardship Consecration Sunday in February, Colonial Hills will be financially on track.

The Futures Committee offers recommendations based on what we call "triggering events." When certain agreed-on indicators become "triggering events," we know it is time to take certain actions.

The Futures Committee joyfully and unanimously submits the following report to be used as a planning guideline by the Administrative Board (Charge Conference) in establishing both immediate and long-range goals and objectives.

The Vision

We envision Colonial Hills allowing the Four Building Blocks to continue to guide our future just as they have in the past twenty years. We reaffirm the level of commitment to Christ and the vital ministry fostered over the years by the Four Building Blocks, which we now ask the Leadership Conference to reaffirm by vote action.

1. **Ministry must be Christ-centered to meet the needs of people, not of the institution.**

We must continue to honor our commitment to one clergy/program staff person for every 100 people in worship or every 300 members, whichever is most advantageous in building the team necessary for networking and development of people relationships. This ratio must be a "trigger" by which we determine when to add or subtract staff.

We must continue to seek from each new member and visitor an answer to the question, "What one thing do you need from your church that we do not have? Tell us, and we'll help you get started."

We must continue to do needs assessments of the city so as to always be addressing the actual spiritual needs of the people.

2. Worship is the initial building block of congregational life, sustained and nurtured by Christian education.

We must continue to place a high emphasis on preaching and music in the life of worship.

We must continue to determine parking, educational, and worship space by using the "trigger" of 80% of capacity. (Determined by 30 sq. feet per person first grade and under, and 20 sq. feet per person second grade and over. Senior adults and children up to first grade must be on first floor only.) We have learned through experience that a reasonable limit of debt service is between 25-30% of the total budget income. This reasonable limit keeps any one aspect of growth from detrimentally impacting other people's needs.

3. God wants the church to grow spiritually and numerically.

We must continue the "Umbrella Concept" which provides the basis for reaching the unchurched wherever they are, physically or spiritually, and nurturing all valid expressions of the Christian faith.

We must continue to accept a leading role as a large church in the connectional system, to include support at District, Conference, Jurisdictional, and General Conference levels, as well as provide extra assistance to smaller churches attempting to grow as we grow.

4. God expects the best from each of us.

The Committed Best Concept should be continued, reinforced, and expanded into every area of the life of the church.

Our evolving understanding of Dollar for Dollar, defined as evangelism, local outreach, and world missions (including Apportionments), must be continued as a major commitment of CHUMC.

CHUMC will demonstrate stewardship by making some

amount of monthly payments to Apportionments after taking care of salaries and bonds.

Developing stewards rather than raising budgets will continue to be the focus of all stewardship endeavors. We will continue to emphasize tithing and percentage giving.

The Finance Committee will: recommend authorized spending in the form of an annual budget based on the results of the stewardship program; seek new sources of income through fund raisers, foundation, and by use of the facilities; i.e., expand day school.

Where We Are Now

The baseline (present status) for evaluating where we are now and what we need to do now to plan our future is:

> 895 family units
> 1,822 members
> 844 worship average
> $943,742 annual budget
> 6¾ Program Staff
> 7½ Support Staff

Based on this baseline, three triggers have already gone off. As of December 1988, we are 1¾ full-time program persons short, and we are out of room in the areas of education and expanded music needs. In addition, our statistics tell us that between 1992-93 we will need to have the use of additional sanctuary space for worshipers.

Recommendations

1. That CHUMC continue to take risks in faith to further God's Kingdom in the name of Jesus Christ.
2. That immediate staff and space requirements (1989) be addressed within the context of the Master Plan and the priority of the triggering events.
3. That people-oriented programs be reaffirmed by the establishment of a program development leader (volunteer layperson) to represent people programs on the Executive Committee.
4. Conduct a three-year building fund drive to raise a minimum of $2 million for the purpose of building the first floor of the three-story multipurpose building, a twelve-hundred-seat

sanctuary, and remodel the present sanctuary, in this order, as needed according to the 80% Growth Principle. The actual cost of the two projects may be more than $2 million. The purpose of the building fund drive is to borrow as little as possible.

The Strategy

1. Begin search for architectural and fund-raising services the week after the Leadership Conference in January 1989.
2. Conduct the campaign in October 1989.
3. Of the $2 million, use $1.5 million up front against the debt itself. The other $500,000, use for debt service of the sanctuary.
4. Begin construction on the multipurpose building first, as soon as the cost of the first floor is on hand.
5. Continue to collect the building-fund money toward the sanctuary. Construction to begin when either the money is in hand or we reach 80% capacity in the largest worship service. Special attention must be given to Christmas Eve, Easter, and how many large Sundays we have each year.
6. It is assumed in this report that beginning in 1989 we will again begin to honor our commitments to Dollar for Dollar and the one staff person for every 100 persons in worship.

The Rationale

1. Allows us to meet both the present educational needs as well as being financially in a position to provide adequate worship space in a timely fashion.
2. Meets the concerns of those who want additional educational space now and those who want to make sure we don't build a new sanctuary until we absolutely need it.
3. Follows closely the intent of the Master Plan.
4. Is the best form of stewardship, in that it is the least expensive and we don't wind up with no use for the present Sanctuary.
5. We have learned from the old choir loft how difficult it is for us to plan to use additional wings where people will not be able to see or to feel a part of the worship service.

The Procedure

At present, there is no money attached to the above motion. Every step of the way, the Administrative Board will have the opportunity to vote on each major expenditure. It is our opinion that both the architect and the fund raiser should be selected and approved by March 1. We anticipate that the decision to hire these two individuals will be done at a church conference and that the details along the way be approved by the Administrative Board.

The Motion

THAT WE: (1) APPROVE THE ABOVE FUTURES COMMITTEE PROPOSAL; (2) AUTHORIZE THE ESTABLISHMENT OF A BUILDING COMMITTEE TO INTERVIEW AND RECOMMEND AN ARCHITECT; (3) IMPOWER THE EXECUTIVE COMMITTEE TO SELECT AND RECOMMEND A PROFESSIONAL FUND RAISER.